Now's the Day, Now's the Hour: Poems for John Maclean

edited by Henry Bell & Joey Simons

NOW'S THE DAY, NOW'S THE HOUR

Poems for John Maclean

Published in 2023 by Tapsalteerie
Tarland, Aberdeenshire
www.tapsalteerie.co.uk

Cover art: a reinterpratation of El Lissitzky's cover design
for 'Wendingen' magazine, Series 6 no. 11, October 1922.

ISBN: 978-1-9162148-9-7

Printed by Imprint Digital, UK

Thanks to Creative Scotland for their help
towards the publication of this collection.

*   *   *

Rights to the work in this anthology remain with the authors, their
estates or publishers. Hamish Henderson's work is included by kind
permission of the Henderson family. We are grateful to Carcanet Press
for permission to reproduce the poetry of Hugh MacDiarmid, Edwin
Morgan and Sorley Maclean. Andrew Tannahill's work is included by the
kind permission of David Jones. Alistair Hulett's work is included with
thanks to the Alistair Hulett Trust. David Morrison's work appears thanks
to the Morrison family. Freddie Anderson's work is reproduced with
the kind permission of Paul Anderson. Archie Hind's work is included
thanks to Sheila Hind. Matt McGinn's work is reproduced with the
permission of Shona McGinn. 'The Fechtin Dominie' appeared in Norlan
Lichts from Rymour Books. 'Strike' by Lola Olufemi is reproduced with
thanks to Hajar Press, Every attempt has been made to find the rights
holders of all other works.

Huge thanks to the families of TS Law and Morris Blythman (Thurso
Berwick) for their permission to include the work of both writers and for
their generous support for this book which is of course is in great part
the labour of those two comrades – alongside countless others.

Henry Bell & Joey Simons

INTRODUCTION

'Now's the day, now's the hour, we must fight capitalism to
death,' wrote John Maclean in 1919. Revolutionary school teacher,
communist organiser, leader of the anti-war movement: John
Maclean was the foremost socialist in the country, and that year
he was determined that a revolution must be begun in Scotland
to defend the revolutions in Russia and Germany. Maclean
believed that a new world could be won and that Scotland must
play its part. It is significant that in this call for an international
revolution Maclean invoked these words of Robert Burns:

> Now's the day, an now's the hour:
> See the front o battle lour,
> See approach proud Edward's power –
> Chains and Slaverie.

In 1919, as he united his ideas of anti-imperialist socialism with a
Scottish communism of the clans, Maclean was deploying 'Scots
Wha Hae' to synthesise the Scottish fight for independence with
the international class war. For Maclean it was clear that Edward's
power – Chains and Slaverie – stemmed now not from English
royalty, but from global capital. In fact Burns himself, though he
wrote 'Scots Wha Hae' as a tribute to Bruce at Bannockburn, had
another hero in mind, writing to his publisher that he 'had no
idea of giving myself any trouble on the subject till the accidental
recollection of that glorious struggle for freedom, associated with
the glowing ideas of some other struggles of the same nature, not
quite so ancient, roused my rhyming mania.' Burns was thinking not of Bruce, but of the radical republican Thomas Muir of

Huntershill who had just been sentenced to exile for the crime of sedition. In Burns's poetry, as in Maclean's rhetoric, the Scottish heroes fight for freedom and become ciphers for each other in the centuries-long battle against the hydra of oppression. Each defeated radical passing the flame on to another.

> By Oppression's woes and pains,
> By your sons in servile chains!
> We will drain our dearest veins,
> But they shall be free.

Maclean too died so others could be free, collapsing one hundred years ago on stage at a cinema in Oatlands, Glasgow. He died on St Andrew's Day, 1923. Years of hard labour, force-feeding, and state persecution had broken him. In his final speeches he railed against the growing threat of fascism, unsafe housing, degrading and dangerous work, police violence, and the hunger and poverty that capitalism forces upon the workers. He warned against the endless wars of the coming century that he knew were inevitable if capitalism was not defeated. From our vantage point we can see how prescient and how essential his warnings were.

That those warnings have come down to us at all is due in no small part to Scotland's poets. In 1948, at a meeting in Glasgow to mark the 25th anniversary of Maclean's death, Hugh MacDiarmid and Sydney Goodsir Smith took to the platform to recite original poems in honour of the great revolutionary. 'Thus as a result of the Scottish literary renaissance which he himself had helped to inspire,' wrote Maclean's daughter, Nan Milton, 'the legend took on a new and immortal form.' In 1968, she founded the John Maclean Society, and the following decade saw a flowering of activity in the lead up to the centenary of Maclean's birth, including plays, exhibitions, conferences, murals, radio programmes, school essay competitions, two biographies and the republication of Maclean's writing and speeches. But out of everything, it was *Homage to John Maclean* (1973), a collection of poems, songs and verse, that for Nan Milton contained 'the very heart of the legend.' This book builds on that original collection with newly commissioned poems from some of Scotland's leading contemporary poets together with selections from a wider open call, and from our own research. The following pages are a testament to the fire that Maclean still inspires in those that wish to rebuild society on a sound economic basis.

Yet how those flames stay stoked is never a simple question. In English, Scots, Gaelic and Orcadian, the poems presented here take up Maclean and his causes in all their multitudes. He appears at once as historical figure, internationalist, patriot, revolutionary, Bolshevik, free-thinker, religious symbol, tragic hero and a vessel for our own hopes and dreams in the class struggle. Where the poets and songwriters of the 1970s tended to find in Maclean a kindred spirit in a specific battle to revive Scotland's independence and its radical traditions, the horizon of today's poets seems at once more personal and more global. Capitalism is 'smashing itself to death in competition, strife and bloodshed, driving millions to perdition,' as Maclean predicted. Yet the great movements capable of overcoming this violence seem, for now, to have receded. Between these two poles, the poet must find their place and change it. The task, wrote the Marxist theatre-maker John McGrath, is 'to relate Maclean's words to their historical context, but pointing them, by way of their defeat at the time, to the consequences of their non-fulfilment today.' We turn to Maclean not for tactics, *realpolitik* or cultural renewal but to fully face up to what lies ahead, and to do so without fear or despair. 'There is nothing frightful about it,' he wrote just days before his death. Or as he was once reported saying: 'Be cheerie, comrades. You never can win a revolution without being cheerie.' The poems in these pages brim with that vital spark of humanity and urgency. We are ready, once again, to join the ranks:

> their bombs and guns
> terrorise
> our democratic
> souls
>
> and still
> just look them in the eyes
> and smile
>
> they can never
> rub us out

(Jim Ferguson, 'A Rebel Life', pg. 97)

At the same time, these poems celebrate how much has already been won, and the lasting achievements of Maclean and his comrades. We have included here poems from five of his contemporaries: Dora Montefiore (1851–1933); Sylvia Pankhurst (1882–1960); John S Clarke (1885–1959); Claude McKay (1889 –1948); and Mary Brooksbank (1897–1978). All lived extraordinary and eventful lives across the movements for women's suffrage, black liberation, socialism and communism; lives marked at all points by poetry and imprisonment. Dora Montefiore and Sylvia Pankhurst both suffered periods of incarceration in Holloway gaol, alongside hundreds of Scottish suffragettes, where they wrote and smuggled out poems. Later, both women worked closely with Maclean, sharing speaking platforms and the pages of *The Call* and *Vanguard* in defence of free speech, the Russian revolution and the unemployed. Pankhurst has left us this moving description of her comrade John Maclean:

> Thick-set, and swarthy as a Neapolitan, he recalled to me irresistibly the thought of a great brown bear. His small eyes dark, and twinkling, his mouth, as he talked, his entire set of white teeth, like a dog, at times playfully opening his mouth in a game, at others drawing his lips back with a snarl. Both expressions were common to him. A kindly fellow, gentle and probably incapable of belligerent action [...] When we saw him a month ago he was holding great meetings and seemed stronger and more confident than ever. Yet he lived the bare lonely life of an ascetic. Parted from his wife and children he lived quite alone, doing his own cooking and housework [...] declaring that 'pease brose' was one of his daily meals. His tone bespoke the cheerful frugality that was only too near to want.

Montefiore witnessed Maclean's return to Glasgow from Peterhead jail and wrote:

> Maclean has descended into Hell, the Hell of the capitalist prison and on the third day he has risen again. His followers, who love him and trust him, have not been scattered abroad, but have gained in insight and in solidarity [...] the fight will go on, and will never cease, until the Red Flag waves, not

only over the City of Glasgow, but from the Clock
Tower of Westminster, as a symbol that the People
have entered into their inheritance.

Their comrade Claude McKay was born in Sunny Ville, Jamaica
before moving to New York in 1914, where he would later play
a leading role in the Harlem Renaissance. There he met the
communist agitator and publisher Max Eastman, editor of *The
Liberator*, where McKay first published his poem 'If We Must
Die'. He next moved to England, and at the International Socialist Club in London met key figures from Glasgow: 'Guy Aldred,
an anarchist editor... [and] Arthur McManus and William
Gallacher, the agitators from the Clyde.' In 1920, he published
a famous letter in Pankhurst's newspaper *Workers' Dreadnought*,
challenging the outright racism of the labour movement against
a background of deadly race riots in British port cities, which
saw dozens of black seamen killed or injured by white mobs.
Shamefully, Gallacher and Emmanuel Shinwell helped spark
the very first of these outrages, which occurred in Glasgow in
January 1919, just days before the far more famous 'Bloody
Friday' of the Battle of George Square. Both leaders had made
speeches in support of a 'colour' bar on Chinese and black
sailors. We have no record of Maclean's writings or speeches
from this period, and he was not in Scotland at the time. The
connection between the harbour riots and the forty hours strike
is one the labour movement has yet to fully reckon with, and
remains a key political question for us today.

Maclean, Pankhurst, Montefiore and McKay were all part
of an international socialist movement that was in constant
dialogue with the most advanced elements of the struggle for a
new world. The pages of newspapers like *The Liberator, Workers'
Dreadnought* and later, *New Times and Ethiopia News*, were filled

not only with reports from uprisings and strikes, but illustrations, cartoons and poetry. They played a particularly important role in developing practical support for anti-colonial movements, and published the work of radical black writers such as McKay and Langston Hughes, alongside pieces from Pankhurst and Maclean, sustained by a mass working-class readership. The movement on Clydeside, as James Kelman has noted, was also remarkable in its diversity. Syndicalists, suffragettes, reformist socialists, Christian socialists, anarchists, anti-parliamentary communists and industrial unionists all played their part in the ferment.

> There may have been sectarianism, political as well as religious, but on the left there was also a general commitment to certain tenets e.g. the anti-war position, universal suffrage, adequate housing, a proper education, healthcare etc. That commitment extended to a common political end and the acceptance of the validity of much Marxian theory. On Clydeside and elsewhere people lived by a set of principles and were prepared to confront the full might of the British State. There were divergences, but the fact remains that for many working class people in Scotland an alternative way of life was on offer. It was not just a matter of economics.*

At the same time, economics, or its critique, played an important role in uniting these diverse political tendencies through a common subscription to the labour theory of value. The popular

---

* Kelman, James, introduction to *Born Up a Close: Memoirs of a Brigton Boy* by Hugh Savage, p.21, Glendaruel, Argyll: Argyll Publishing

understanding that workers produce wealth and capitalists appropriate it was to have an enduring effect on the form of socialism that took root on the Clyde, and Maclean himself stated that his 'greatest crime' was 'the teaching of Marxian economics to the Scottish workers.' Alongside the widespread reviling of landlords, the basic principle that the producers had a right to the fruits of their labour formed a central tenet in a galaxy of working-class activity on Clydeside. Through factory organising, tenement committees, street meetings, pipe bands, Marxist education, socialist Sunday schools, mass demonstrations, industrial strikes, imprisonment and militant direct action, Maclean and his comrades unleashed an energy that helped generations of people in Scotland to understand their class interests and periodically shake the bastions of political and economic power. From the rent strikers and peace crusaders of 1915 to the international brigadiers of the 1930s; from the Tramp's Trust and the unemployed movements of the 1920s to the Upper Clyde Shipbuilders and Lee Jeans occupations of the 1970s and 1980s; from the Glasgow Girls of the early 2000s to the surrounding of the deportation van on Kenmure Street in 2021, these movements could not have emerged without imaginative knowledge of our past victories and collective strength. Indeed, both contemporaneously and since, these movements were all imagined within the prism of 'Red Clydeside.'

As this book shows, poetry remains the red thread we use to stitch together these moments of history and make sense of the present. For Crystal Eastman, in a portrait of Maclean, Gallagher and others published in *The Liberator* in October 1919, 'the best thing about these labour leaders of the new order [was] their love of poetry.' The cultural commitments of the early 20th century labour movement, together with Maclean's dedication to learning, are again finding their reflection today in the Workers'

Stories Project, the Red Sunday School, and the Popular Education Network. In Glasgow and elsewhere, the combined efforts of urban redevelopment, deindustrialisation, official neglect and outright suppression mean that now more than ever must we make a conscious effort to maintain the transmission belts of radical memory.

> They are taking it apart now
> the school where he used to teach night classes
> making Celtic communism contagious
> naming capitalism so that we could see out of it.
> Great pieces of stone are lying, heavy, rosy
> and a right pile of mess behind them.

(Beth Frieden, 'The teacher and the school', pg. 28)

The City Fathers are happy to watch these buildings crumble, and not only the masonry. Remarkably few traces of our history are acknowledged in the landscape of Scotland's cities, where the statues and street names are given over to slavers and aristocrats. Those that do exist – the Maclean cairn in Pollokshaws; the Mary Barbour statue in Govan; the memorials to the International brigadiers in Glasgow and Motherwell; the Chilean Solidarity monument in East Kilbride – do so only thanks to popular efforts. We may now add one more. On the centenary of Maclean's death, a specially-commissioned stained glass window, designed by the artist Keira Maclean, will be unveiled. The window itself is not a memorial, but a dialogical tool; an open-ended discussion between the many influences on Maclean's life and his own influence on the city around him. Opposite the ruins of Pollokshaws arcade, a stone's throw from where Maclean grew up, it will light up the learning of a new generation of Glasgow's citizens.

On the other side of the library's walls, the fight today is the same as when Maclean died. The demands he set out in his final election address for the Scottish Workers' Republican Party are our own: the prevention of evictions; safe and well-equipped houses for all; decent food and clothing; control over our workplaces; an end to police violence; anti-imperialist solidarity; and the revolutionary transformation of Scotland and the world into a society in which no one person's life may lessen another and 'social murder or warfare shall vanish forever.' As Beth Frieden writes, 'we are all dreaming of the future.' Whether the poems here were written over a hundred years ago or yesterday: there's much to do while we're awake. 'Until developments are ripe for a great mass movement,' Maclean's address ended, 'our party considers it right and proper to take part in the everyday struggle of our class for a sufficient allowance of food, clothing, shelter, education, and leisure, and in the defence of members of our class unjustly treated.'

And so Maclean's legacy lives on politically. But more so than perhaps any other Scottish figure – save Bonnie Prince Charlie – his legacy lives on in song and poetry. Maclean's unique fusion of Marxism, Scottish and Gaelic identity, and passionate internationalism have seen him sow the seeds for generations of socialist, communist and anarchist poets on these islands in the northeast Atlantic. Morris Blythman (Thurso Berwick) and TS Law, the great working-class poets, singers, organisers and educators who first assembled the original material for this book in 1973, commented that 'in the matter of who do we remember and how do we remember them, poets always have the last word.'

We would add to this and borrow from Alasdair Gray in saying that Maclean allowed workers and poets to live imaginatively in Scotland, and that artists return to him precisely for that sustenance. He presented a glimpse of another world and another Scotland that continues to inspire. It is his revolutionary vision of what Scotland can and should be – a country held in common, governed by the workers, and working internationally for solidarity and peace – that continues to be sung and painted, performed, and enacted in rooms all over this country. As part of the Maclean Centenary this year we will see actors exploring his life at Platform in Easterhouse, musicians singing the songs of this book in the Royal Concert Hall at Celtic Connections, a conference at Glasgow University, Marxist evening classes in his memory led by the Popular Education Network, a songwriting competition, the annual march from his grave, a poster competition across Scottish schools, an exhibition in the Mitchell Library, the aforementioned memorial window in Pollokshields, new artworks by Ruth Ewan and Isobel Neviazsky, and this book that you hold in your hands. In Maclean we find a guide who, as Harry Josephine Giles says, is 'a sowel at tried, a sowel at held tae revolution.' A soul who, as Hugh MacDiarmid wrote, was 'both beautiful and red.'

Naomi Mitchison posited that Maclean was gripping because he was a mythic 'king of Strathclyde' who died for his people. Maclean was a martyr. In his poem 'On John Maclean' Edwin Morgan remarked that 'failures may be interesting' and he is right, but more than that, the poetry and politics here tell us that failures are vital, we cannot move forward without them. As the Filipina revolutionary Salub Algabre wrote:

> We did what we ourselves had decided upon – as free people, and power resides in the people. What we did was our heritage... We decided to rebel, to rise up and strike down the sources of power. No uprising fails. Each one is a step in the right direction.

Our struggles and our defeats give meaning to our future. And more than anywhere it is in poetry and song that we, the people, can explore that past and that future. A future that is already glimpsed here by a century of Scotland's finest poets and singers. We publish this work not just as a tribute to Maclean but also as a tribute to his countless comrades, and in the hope that the singing of the songs about their struggle will continue to fuel the fight for a Scotland free from both capitalism and the British state.

THE TOP AND HEM OF OUR STORY

To make wealth rapidly, capitalists have wrought men and women and children long hours at high speed and for wages that just keep them alive. Here the class struggle begins with the desire to steal the maximum from the workers. The workers feel the necessity for united effort, so that they may resist the attacks of the enemy, the capitalists. Trade Unions are formed and the strike is used to get as much of the wealth produced as possible. But wives and children starve and the unions must yield. Though united, the workers still fight an unequal battle...

That the class struggle is bitter we need only reckon the annual death toll of the workers, the maimed, the poisoned, the physically wrecked by overwork, the mentally wrecked by worry, and those forced to suicide by desperation. It is a more bloody and more disastrous warfare than that to which the soldier is used. Living in slums, breathing poisonous and carbon-laden air, wearing shoddy clothes, eating adulterated and life-extinguishing food, the workers have greater cause for a forcible revolution than had the French capitalists in 1789.

 — *John Maclean, letter to Pollokshaws News, 1902*

Somhairle MacGill-Eain (Sorley MacLean)

CLANN GHILL-EAIN / CLAN MACLEAN

Chan e iadsan a bhàsaich
an àrdan Inbhir-Chèitein,
dh'aindeoin gaisge is uabhair,
ceann uachdrach ar sgeula;
ach esan bha 'n Glaschu,
ursann-chatha nam feumach,
Iain mòr MacGill-Eain,
ceann is fèitheam ar sgeula.

* * *

Not they who died
in the hauteur of Inverkeithing,
in spite of valour and pride,
the high head of our story,
but he who was in Glasgow
the battlepost of the poor,
great John Maclean,
the top and hem of our story.

Hamish Henderson

THE JOHN MACLEAN MARCH

Hey Mac did ye see him as he cam' doon by Gorgie,
    Awa ower the Lammerlaw or north o' the Tay?
Yon man is comin', and the haill toon is turnin' oot:
    We're a' shair he'll win back tae Glesgie the day.
The jiners and hauders-on are marchin' frae Clydebank,
    Come noo an' hear him – he'll be ower thrang tae byde.
Turn oot, Jock and Jimmie: leave yer crans an' yer muckle gantries.

    Great John Maclean's comin' back tae the Clyde.
    Great John Maclean's comin' back tae the Clyde.

Argyle Street and London Road's the route that we're marchin' –
    The lads frae the Broomielaw are oot – tae a man.
Hey, Neil, whaur's yer hadarums, ye big Hielan teuchter?
    Get yer pipes, mate, and march at the heid o' the clan.
Hullo Pat Malone: sure I knew ye'd be here, so:
    The red and the green lad, we'll wear side by side,
The Gorbals is his the day and Glesgie belangs tae him.

    Ay, Great John Maclean's comin' hame tae the Clyde,
    Great John Maclean's comin' hame tae the Clyde,

Forward tae Glesgie Green we'll march in guid order:
    Wull grips his banner weel (that boy isna blate).
Aye there, man, that's Johnnie noo – that's him, there,
    the bonnie fechter.

Lenin's his fiere, lad, and Leibknecht's his mate.
Tak tent when he's speakin' for, they'll mind whit wis said here
    In Glesgie, oor city – an' the haill warld beside.
Och hey, lad, the scarlet's bonnie: here's tae ye Hielan' Shony!

    Oor John Maclean has come hame to the Clyde.
    Oor John Maclean has come hame to the Clyde.

Aweel, when it's feenished, I'm awa back tae Springburn,
    (Come hame tae yer tea, John, we'll sune hae ye fed).
It's hard work the speakin': och I'm shair he'll be tired the nicht.
    I'll sleep on the flair, Mac, and gie John the bed.
The haill city's quiet noo: it kens that he's restin'
    At hame wi' his Glesgie freens, their fame and their pride!
The red will be worn, my lads, an' Scotland will march again

    Noo great John Maclean has come hame tae the Clyde.
    Great John Maclean has come hame tae the Clyde.

David Betteridge

JAGGILY

for Bob Starrett, political cartoonist

Friend, your bramble's thorns are sharp
as sharp. Whoever thinks to pick the fruit –
your drawing makes the point –
will run the risk of hurt.
As well as thorns, and leaves,
your penwork's densities of black on white
convey the thickened stems of older growth
in stark, dark contrast to the new.
Stiff now, and hard to push aside,
they give the tendrils of fresh green
a palisade of strength,
and skyward pathways to pursue.

This sketch you've sent
I've pinned on my study wall. There,
with Luxemburg close by, and Spartacus, and Parks,
and those who breached the Winter Palace gates,
and all the folk of UCS, and John Maclean,
above them all your bramble clambers
jaggily.

A comfort and discomfort,
it's a spur to action in the cause –
unfinished but continuing –
that we, along with millions, love
and cannot help but love,
implacably.

Sheila Templeton

THE FECHTIN DOMINIE

I am not here, then, as the accused; I am here as the accuser of
capitalism dripping with blood from head to foot.
– John Maclean's Speech from the Dock, 1918.

Ahint yer hearse they githered that December day
nummers niver seen since syne in Glesga, twinty thoosan
mebbe mair – steppin oot the lang road tae Eastwood,
tackety buits an dainty sheen in the seelence o frosty air.

Aabody claimed ye fir their ain, sauls thirsty fir learnin. Ye set them
     ableeze
gied them new een, new warlds; *Celtic Communism*, votes fir weemen,
the feenish o colonial pooer, modren noshuns tae bring back the auld
     wyes –
yer black een fair skinklin, wirds wyvin sic truth, kittlin up brave herts.

An mak a difference ye did. Reed Clydeside set oan its road
yer speech fae the dock eissed tae this day,
a set text fir socialism; a hunner year syne, yer face
oan 4 Kopec postage – but yer stamp oan Scotland foriver.

An wis it wirth the cost, John Maclean? Peterheid jile, that rubber tube
sickenin doon yer thrapple, puir fushenless lungs, fite hair at 40;
Agnes an yer quinies awa fan they cudna stamach anither day
o makkin-dae, niver eneuch siller. Yer ain licht oot at 44.

I jalouse ye'd say there wis nae chyce – naethin else for it.
This wis aye the darg set oot for ye, the darg yer starnies sung.

Beth Frieden

AN TIDSEAR AGUS AN SGOIL

Tha iad ga toirt a-mach às a chèile a-nis
a' bunsgoil far an do chùm e clasaichean oidhche
a' dèanamh comannachd Ceilteach gabhaltach,
ag ainmeachadh calpachas gus am faiceamaid a-mach às.
Tha pìosan mòra cloiche nan laighe, tomadach ròsach
agus sgrios mòr air an cùlaibh.

'S e tàmailt a th' ann, tàmailt, is an aon rud math –
gu bheil sinn uile aontaichte
chan eil duine san sgìre toilichte ma dheidhinn
(cho bòidheach sa bha an togalach! ars esan)
(chaidh mise dhan sgoil an sin, ars ise)
ach chan ann leinne ri ràdh,
chan eil duine a' faighneachd oirnne;
chan eil smachd againn air an àrainneachd mun cuairt oirnn.

Ceud bliadhna às dèidh Iain Mòr MacGillEathain,
's dòcha nach aithneachar ainm air an sgafail
neo am measg na h-oigridh a' cluich ri thaobh
ach cha tèid na bruadairean seo a sgrios
agus cha chuir tobhta eile an t-eagal oirnne.

Le gach clach air a leigeil,
tha beachd às dèidh beachd
air saoradh, a' sireadh aoidheachd ùr
agus a-nis tha sinn uile a' bruadair
mun àm ri teachd ann an dòigh
ris nach robh sinn an dùil
a' dùsgadh sa mhadainn is ceist oirnn
a bheil barrrachd ann ri buannachadh.

Nach tèid sinn, Pollokshaws, air ais
gu comannachd; air adhart
gu comannachd!
Nach tèid?

THE TEACHER AND THE SCHOOL

They are taking it apart now
the school where he used to teach night classes
making Celtic communism contagious
naming capitalism so that we could see out of it.
Great pieces of stone are lying, heavy, rosy
and a right pile of mess behind them.

It's a disgrace, an embarrassment, and the only good thing –
we are all agreed
that no one here is happy about it
(such a beautiful building! he said)
(I went to school here, she said)
but it isn't up to us,
nobody asked us;
we do not have control of our environment.

One hundred years after Great John Maclean
maybe his name would not be recognised on the scaffold
or amongst the youth playing beside it
but these dreams cannot be demolished
and we are not afraid of one more ruin.

With every stone loosened,
idea after idea
is freed to seek a new home
and now we are all dreaming
about the future in a way
we were not expecting
waking up in the morning
wondering if there is not more to be won.

Will we not go, Pollokshaws, back
to communism; forward
to communism!
Will we not?

Joey Simons

DIALECTIC DYAD

dialectic dyad
camarade

yaddayadda
camarada

make a wish
tovarisch

hide and seek
al rafiq

sail the sea
tongzhi

root canal
heval

push the barra
a chara

      to the barricade
      comrade

      tailor-made
      comrade

      forever weighed
      comrade

        never betrayed
        comrade

        always afraid
        comrade

osc

        ill

                    ate

comrade

        oscillate

neither good nor bad
neither happy nor sad

always a myriad
comrade

        add

add

                    add

WE BETTER GO UNDER FIGHTING TOGETHER

All the fortnight we have dozed and read lazily novels. In fact it has been the laziest holiday I have ever spent [...] We intend to break the bank at Monte Carlo. You will marry a millionaire yet my dear. If my purse were in proportion to my love for you I certainly would. However if the millions don't come we shall try, won't we dearest, to make love cover all the defects otherwise. How I have been longing for you all the voyage and how I begin to weary till Xmas when we shall be locked away in one another's arms for the rest of our dual existence. My word how happy we shall be, we two, with an Italian sky of joy unalloyed over our heads.

    – *John Maclean, letter to Agnes, August 9th, 1909*

I'm sure your mother will have told you I'm free again [...] I was so very very sorry that the wicked men who kept me a prisoner wouldn't let you in to see me [...] I've heard wonderful stories how you are both growing so big, and I'm just a wee bit afraid that if you don't come home soon, I won't know you! [...] I was amused to read Jean's letter where she said she was going back only to Julius Caesar in history. That's right Jean, tell your teacher about Wells' great History of the World, and how your father took you back two hundred thousand years before Julius Caesar was born at all [...] I'll write again soon, but you have both to write me a right good letter each, or I'll come through and gobble you up like the angry ogre...

    – *John Maclean, letter to Nan and Jean on release from prison,*
      October 26th, 1922

My dearest Agnes,

(I received your extra-welcome letter alright and have just got Nan's interesting, well-written, well-composed and amusing one as well)

The only hope of economic security (of a kind) at present is from the masses. And so I must ever keep in the fight. I am therefore standing again in the Gorbals.

Now any chance I have of holding my own against the deluge of Labour Party lies against me at the next election, e.g. that I was in the pay of the Moderates, your absence from me, etc, is your immediate return home and appearance in public with me.

If you cannot come I'll be blackened worse than ever and I will be economically damned. If that is so, I have made up my mind for the worst, that we'll not come together again. If I go down, I must go down with my flag at the mast-top. Nothing on earth can shift me from that. Now there's the tragedy for you, as clearly and bluntly as I can put it.

If it is your duty to be here, as I maintain it now is, I contend it is your duty to stand shoulder to shoulder with me in the hardest and dirtiest battle of my life. If we have to go under we better go under fighting together than fighting one another.

Realising that this is the greatest crisis in our lives I cannot find words to say more.

If you come I'd prefer you to come at once and walk right in.

Whatever course we follow, remember that you are the only woman I love, and can ever love. x

Your loving husband,

Johnnie xxx

    – *John Maclean, last letter to Agnes, September 14ᵗʰ, 1923*

Alistair Hulett

JOHN MACLEAN AND AGNES WOOD

John Maclean and Agnes Wood were lovers twa within one bower
She gi'ed him strength tae carry on when he gaed through his darkest
  hour

John was cast intae prison strang for speakin oot in the fight for peace
And it fell doon tae Agnes Wood tae raise the cry for his release

When he came hame tae a hero's welcome she thocht the nightmare
  was at an end
But John resolved tae sodger on and though she begged him he
  wadna bend

Said Agnes Wood tae John Maclean, I lo'e ye dear as I lo'e my life
But if ye'll no' be a husband tae me I'll no' continue tae be yer wife

Agnes this thing that ye demand is mair nor ocht than I e'er could gi'e
Scotland's cry for revolution tak's higher place than my love for thee

If Scotland's cry for revolution tak's higher place than yer love for me
Till fishes fly and seas run dry ye'll ha'e nae mair o' my company

And slowly, slowly she's got up and slowly she's gone doon the stair
John cried oot in grief and woe, fareweel my ain love forever mair

John hit the street like a tornado, fower years he burned like a
  shooting star
Hands off Ireland! Hands off Russia! Then he fell in wi' Erskine
  of Marr

Erskine of Marr was a high born noble, won ower by chance tae
the workers' cause
Less like a tree than a leaf in autumn that's tossed aboot by ony
wind that blaws

Thus lesser men gained Lenin's ear and syne became Lenin's
gramophone
The mair John tried tae rail against them the mair he found they
had ears of stone

By 1920 he's back in prison a twelve month stretch wi' the young
McShane
When John came oot McShane was gone, noo Red Clyde's hero
was a' his lane

Ostracised by his former comrades, driven deep into poverty
John turned once mair tae his ain dear Agnes, I need ye noo love
if ye need me

Oh John my man, I could ne'er refuse ye. I've waited lang for this
very day
And she's come hame tae her ain guid man, and in his airms she
gladly lay

But o'er three months were passed and ower, cauld winds of
death gart these lovers pairt
His dochter Nan did proudly scrieve, 'They broke his body but
not his hairt'

Henry Bell

ON MORALITY

I am waiting on the corner of Vicky Road and Allison Street
to meet the man who first told me about Maclean,
one hungover morning in a Partick flat.

That morning when the sun bounced off the grime:
windows grey with bus exhaust, casting a moth-eaten light.
My friend had slept with his shoes on.
In the morning he paced the room, with black coffee
and the story of Maclean on his breath.
He told me how Maclean, Lenin, Gramsci
had all glimpsed the future and shown us the way
to storm heaven.

I've got £30 in my pocket for him now,
that's why we're meeting here, twelve years on.
I want to see how he is, and he needs cash.
There's no one much about and I worry
every time someone comes by looking broken.

Maclean said there were two moralities.
What is moral for the ruling class
is totally immoral for the working class.

My friend comes up the road, using his bike as a crutch,
and a cross. He's broken both his legs.
I hand him the money straight away so no one is left unsure.
And we talk, or maybe I listen, to stories
about people left behind, trapped in hotels,
seeking refuge, trying to mend and beg and steal.

What is moral for the working class
is totally immoral for the ruling class.

I think of my friend in a green parka
at the head of a great swell of people
charging down the Gallowgate,
his arms out gallus
and his voice loud but hoarse:
'Bullshit, come off it!
The enemy is profit!'

There is a divine violence that is law-destroying
a violence that frees us, restores us
a momentary and terrible violence
that is totally immoral for the ruling class.
And there is a grinding, soul crushing violence,
that steals lives by inches, breaks legs
and seals up doors and windows;
the thousand year violence
that is totally immoral for us.

My friend shakes my hand
on the corner by the squarey park.
He's away to help some wee guy.
This money will make all the difference,
he says. He breathes heavily
and places his weight down through his forearm
onto the bike's handlebars, lifts himself and wheels off:
a shadow in the lamplight
still on his way to storm heaven.

William Letford

WORKING

Ten quick years had passed since I'd last worked with
my father. During those years, to save what was left of
his knees, he'd retired. If poetry could be said to have a
pit face, that's where I'd been, scraping by. I was slightly
surprised by the phone call but we're at the stage now
where time spent together is significant. And true enough
if you clean the gutters on my parents' house, there is a
tricky spot behind the satellite dish. He picked a clear
Wednesday when the sky was crisp. September for me
(past summer). November for my father (approaching
winter). There's a rough skill in carrying a three-piece
ladder. It's weight and balance should be pressed against
the shoulder. The steady heft of it returned an important
comfort I'd forgotten. When you work for your family
roofing business, the sweat on your back falls as food
on their table. How sad, and how beautiful, that this day
we weren't working for money, or food, we were working
for the memories themselves. I was careful when I
got to roof height. The friction, some would call it faith,
between the bottom of the ladder and the concrete below
was troubling me. I was reaching past the satellite dish
to remove a clump of turf sprouting from the downpipe
when my father shouted, Do you know the best place to find
a meteor is in the gutter of your house? I stopped stretching
and leant back in to look down at him. Micrometeors,
fragments of meteorites that break up in the atmosphere
and land on your roof and get washed into the gutter by the
rain. He cleared his throat. So stop fidgeting like you're feart

and get your hand in there. You're scooping up the universe.
Retirement had extended his boundaries. And like magic,
the fistful of mulch I removed from the downpipe had a
new sparkle. Rather than place the universe into the pail.
I let it continue its journey downward where it landed,
with an unexpectedly heavy slap, across my father's back.
When he looked up, the mud splattered across his shoulder
made his smile so much brighter. Whether you're fixing a roof
or working at the pit face of poetry, we must repair ourselves
daily, turning everything that's thrown at us into hope.

Hannah Lavery

OUR HEROES DIE

for John Maclean

He died on
St Andrews Day

My father
& this man

I learnt about him
from all their half
rememberings.

His name uttered
like incantation
by drinking pals –

*The Hero of the
Red Clydeside*

For my father –

a procession
of the wounded

followed him
to his grave.

In crematorium
his children

stood by him
in exile.

A piper,
played the haar in.

We sang.

We sang
We sang
We sang

In unison, we sang –
our starlings murmuration –
a fleeting congress.

Maggie Rabatski

CEUMAN-COISE AN LEATHANAICH

Bha coiseachd nad fhuil:
nach do cheumnaich do sheanmhair
leis a' phàiste do mhàthair
a' mhòr-chuid den astar
à Loch Abar gu ruig Glaschu,
goirt-chasach is acrach,
's a' chaora ghallda a' brodachadh
air fearann an sinnsir.

Beag agadsa dusan mìle san latha air chois
gu foghlam colaiste, ged 's coltach
gun tàinig am fìor ionnsachaidh
air an t-slighe fhèin –
seachad air factaraidhean is gàrraidhean-iarainn,
tro ghlaodhraich iargalta is smùidean puinnseanach
cor-obrach an fheadhainn bha rin cosnadh annt',
is cùiltean grod teis-meadhan a' bhaile
far na shìn iad ri cadal an-fhoiseil.

Is dhìreadh tu mu dheireadh a-mach
gu èadhar glan craobhach Khelvingrove,
taighean-mòra leòmach
a' cleith a' bhrùidealachd a thog iad;
d' uile cheum ribheid às ùr nad chinnt
nach fhuasgladh grèim-bàis nan ceannard
air cumhachd is maoin
gus an oidichear an luchd-obrach,

's a sheasadh iad an guaillibh a chèile
ag iarraidh gu pongail an cuid cheart fhèin –
an searmon leis an do shiubhail do bhròg
fad is farsaing.

Iomchaidh gu bheilear a' coiseachd
nad ainm fhathast, brataichean is òrain,
caithream dearg nan druma
a' tachdadh car treiseag
bleadraich chealgach
sionnaich Westminster.

Harry Josephine Giles

INGLE

Whit uiss a hero? A'm follit plenty
doun glaikit rodds, led plenty
intae gateless wids. A'm sung plenty
sorry sangs fer aefauld kempers
at's brave blades is bricklan nou
aneath the ranks o sitka spruce.
A'm dillt plenty harrs i' the hairts
o fowk at teuk the wird o fowk
at stuid afore the crood, prood
o naebdy but thirsels. Plenty

tae say: here wis a sowel at tried,
a sowel at held tae revolution
lik a ice climber tae a shairp aix,
lik a fantan bairn tae a cheese piece,
like a shewster tae a strecht seam;
plenty tae ken there wis aince a sowel
at felt as thoo did, failt as thoo did,
fowt as thoo did, teuk tent o the fire,
the ae fire thoo're beetan nou,
till aizles turn tae leal flame.

FIRESIDE

What use is a hero? I've followed enough
down foolish roads, led enough
into trackless woods. I've sung enough
sorry songs for righteous heroes
whose brave blades are crumbling now
beneath the ranks of sitka spruce.
I've soothed enough scars in the hearts
of those who took the word of those
who stood before the crowd, proud
of no-one but themselves. Enough

to say: here was a soul who tried,
a soul who held to revolution
like an ice climber to a sharp axe,
like a hungry child to a crust of bread,
like a seamstress to a straight seam;
enough to know there was once a soul
who felt as you did, failed as you did,
fought as you did, looked after the fire,
the same fire you're feeding now,
till embers turn to faithful flame.

Farquhar McLay

THE HUNTERS

It's easy to befriend the dead.
The spent bullet is anyone's
as long as it missed the mark, that is.

The hunters will make it their property.
For the moral will prove too good to lose.

'He won no prizes, I'll be bound,'
they'll say.

They'll question the ground on which he stood
They'll hint at a rather unsteady hand.

'Not Clynes as mill-hand, ten years old,
not John Burns in his red flag days,
not Ramsay the starveling pedagogue,
not even McGovern in his youth
nor the Paisley mechanic Gallacher
fired with so little guile,' they'll say.

And they'll pity the poor tyro then.

He'll be their companion in the field,
a comfort when the bag is bare.
'Couldn't judge distances, you see.
Couldn't bide his time, a man like that,
as all good hunters must,' they'll say.

So easy to befriend the dead,
mould in half-truths the image we will,
accomplish in him our own design.

For John would let the bird fly free,
the hunters he went out to kill.

Jackie Kay

THE SHOES OF DEAD COMRADES

On my father's feet are the shoes of dead comrades.
Gifts from the comrades' sad red widows.
My father would never see good shoes go to waste.
Good brown leather, black leather, leather soles.
Doesn't matter if they're a size too big, small.

On my father's feet are the shoes of dead comrades.
The marches they marched against Polaris. UCS.
Everything they ever believed tied up with laces.
A cobbler has replaced the sole, the heel.
Brand new, my father says, look, feel.

On my father's feet are the shoes of dead comrades.
These are in good nick. These were pricey.
Italian leather. See that. Lovely.
He always was a classy dresser was Arthur.
Ever see Wullie dance? Wullie was a wonderful waltzer.

On my father's feet are the shoes of dead comrades.
It scares me half to death to consider
that one day it won't be Wullie or Jimmy or Arthur,
that one day someone will wear the shoes of my father,
the brown and black leather of all the dead comrades.

SUCH EDUCATION AS WILL MAKE REVOLUTIONISTS

Many people are horrified to hear it said that the working-class standpoint in economics is bound to be different from that of the capitalist. These tender beings dream of a certain 'impartial' social science bringing about the reconciliation of the hostile classes, as if it were possible to avoid taking sides on economic questions in a society in which the interests of the workers are sharply opposed to those of the employers, the needs of tenants conflict with those of the house-owners, and so on. True, the professors of political economy in the universities claim to be impartial men of science. But nobody believes them: their attitude is recognised as a necessary, professional pose. Their teaching has become a mere system of apologetics, by means of which they reveal the moral reasons that justify the plundering of the working class [...] The workers, if they are successfully to resist increased exploitation, and to make progress towards freedom, can only do so if they utilise their resources widely for the training of leaders and the diffusion of essential knowledge amongst themselves.

- A plea for a Labour College for Scotland, *Pamphlet published in February 1916, John Maclean & J. D. MacDougall*

In this respect we differ from the Workers' Educational Association, which simply has for its object the creation of intelligent workers. Personally, I wish to see all opportunities for self-development opened up to the working class. But I am specially interested in such education as will make revolutionists [...] The Scottish Labour College, supported by the British Socialist Party and Independent Labour Party, will be responsible for at least a dozen large classes in Lanarkshire, Glasgow and Clydeside [...] Where classes cannot be held, it is to be hoped that groups will be formed in workshops, at mealtimes and in houses or halls after work-time, to read together and discuss the smaller works of Marx and Engels, and those of well-known Marxian scholars. The Russian revolution was buttressed by city workers thoroughly educated in Marxism. Marxian education, that is independent working-class education, must be the supreme effort of workers this winter.

The greatest 'crime' I have committed in the eyes of the British government and the Scottish capitalist class has been the teaching of Marxian economics to the Scottish workers. That was evident at my 'trial'; that dictated Lord Strathclyde's sentence of three years. Nevertheless, I mean to spend every evening this winter in teaching economics. And every reader should push ahead as a teacher or as a student, and in the active organising of classes...

– *'Independence in working-class education', John Maclean,* The Call, *20 September 1917*

Matt McGinn

DOMINIE, DOMINIE

CHORUS:
Dominie, Dominie
There was nane like John Maclean,
The fighting Dominie.

Tell me where ye're gaun lad, and who ye're gaun to meet –
I'm headed for the station that's in Buchanan Street,
I'll join 200,000 that's there to meet the train
That's bringing back to Glasgow our own dear John Maclean:

Tell me whaur he's been, lad, and why has he been there?
They've had him in the prison for preaching in the Square,
For Johnny held a finger at all the ills he saw,
He was right side o' the people, but he was wrong side o' the law:

Johnny was a teacher in one of Glasgow's schools;
The golden law was silence but Johnny broke the rules,
For a world o' social justice young Johnny couldnae wait,
He took his chalk and easel to the men at the shipyard gate:

The leaders o' the nation made money hand o'er fist
By grinding down the people by the fiddle and the twist,
Aided and abetted by the preacher and the press –
John called for revolution and he called for nothing less:

The bosses and the judges united as one man
For Johnny was a danger to their '14–'18 plan,
They wanted men for slaughter in the fields of Armentiers,
John called upon the people to smash the profiteers:

They brought him to the courtroom in Edinburgh toun,
But still he didnae cower, he firmly held his ground,
And stoutly he defended his every word and deed,
Five years it was his sentence in the jail at Peterheid:

Seven months he lingered in prison misery
Till the people rose in fury, in Glasgow and Dundee,
Lloyd George and all his cronies were shaken to the core,
The prison gates were opened, and John was free once more.

Marianne Tambini

CHILDREN AT DRILL 1916

Photos show kids at drill
Hands on hips
Feet neat
A grid – no touching
In the schoolyard, in the hall,
In any space big enough to hold them
All together.
Left knees bend and bodies tilt
Faces blurred
but concentration discernible
The point was to learn to move in ways
that you are told to move
But you see there is such a Synchronicity
Togetherness
that cannot be crushed
The point was to take Glasgow for milking
of its skill, folk and deep energies
But what the bosses didn't realise was
formations aren't for killing they're for dance

Maryanne Hartness

THE REIGN OF JOHN MACLEAN

It was held high by
proud workers, whose
blood swiftly

pumped through many
optimistic valves, churched
carefully in class

free development, this
red theoretical revolution
provoked, then cut through

precisely, with a celts firm
edge, robust politics,
economics, all so

interdependent, his
were deep set, grounded
in a fairer future.

TS Law

A CYCLE O MACLEANS *(extract)*

I.
S'ant Major Maclean

I hae kent Macleans: the furst I hae in mynd
a schuil janitor we aye caad Mister Maclean.

Familiaritie wi him bred nane
o thon auld nonsense aboot contempt. He was
S'ant Major Maclean, as wuiden-faced, as straucht
as a stout stab i the grund, nae stookie tho, but sherp,
thin-lippit, tongue tripplin as quick as the glent o his een:
smert sodger. 'About turn' he wuid say, an birl,
as jimp as a pooter peerie, peare-kistit hissel.

At the Christmas pairtie at the schuil, ben wuid step
Maclean, beezed-up an gallus as the six
brave colours in the garb o a dacent bard,
an strampin brawlie the lenth o the lang schuilhaa,
his ceremonials a paper glengairrie
wi streamers fleein fae it, and ower his shoother
a chair upsyde doon as bagpype the-tyme he garred
neb-music tirl as tho the pype itsel
was in his thrapple, thon soond the dirl an dunt
o the heidarim-hodarum o his young recruitment
yon day whan Maclean was the pryde o the paerochen,
sap-wuid i the shaves tae groove an set i the roond
an runes o the regimental years until

he stuid hard, strenthie, king o the wuids amang
the thinned-oat growthe the Passchendaele plorie made
o the lave o the singing youth o the Scottish forest.

Athooten regimentals, tho, he was
a corner-stab o a man: and the bairns as kent it.

Wuiden heidit as weel as wuiden-faced! The bairns
wuid say naither eechie nor ochie anent him, kennin
the honestie o wuid is no byordnar.
Nocht else aboot the man is byordnar aither;
he stuid his grund i the weire, and didnae rin,
but didnae faa lik his paer waanchancie fieres,
an bidd as thrawn as John Maclean hissel
whaa stuid an focht oor ain lang weire, but fell
because he naither was the man tae rin.

II.
John Maclean, Republican

The reevolutiounarie thing
aboot Maclean was that he kent
whit he was daein was whit he meant,
an did it lik a sang tae sing.

He was nae rebel gane aglye
lik the coonter-reevolutiounarie
whaa kens wi sic a sair oncairrie
his maister's rascal-tascal py
aye tells him whit he'll no be daein,

an cannae tho he pech an pant
lik onie grampus; mowt an mant
as he may, he speils reactioun, sayin,
'This here fae you I'll tak for me,
that thare I'll gie tae him fae you,
thon thonder tae for him the noo,
and aa thir here tae me I'll gie;
gae lowp an rin the haill day thru.'
Watch oot for him the horallie bairn:
a steerin laud's a stacherin man;
he'll con ye an pawn ye as shuin as he can;
he'll spyle ye an jyle ye in mortar and airn.

It's up the road and dae's ye're telt,
an back again an gasp and gape;
it's beg an bou, an scart and scrape,
an for the boss caa oot yer melt.

Tho we are aften bellowses
whan yokit tae rebellioun's braes,
Maclean sklimmed on wi stuidie pace,
an did his devoirs aa his days,
an didnae staun baith blate an sweir
bi gushet-heid twaa wys tae rin
but gaed the causey croon abuin
or else i the middis o the square.

Andrew Tannahill

RED STAR

Frae auld man's een I'm dichtin bairnie's tears,
As mindfu hou you kythed in khaki claes
When aff we gaed to fecht wi fremit faes:
Scule freens. Lang deid and yerdit wi the years!
In solist herts we happit doutes and fears.
Reformist cuifs had conscience stounds thae days:
Our cause was theirs, they deaved our lugs wi praise;
But fecht's nae place for folk that hae careers.

Our umwhile 'reds' hae Steenie's howf for hame:
Ae man there was that put their shams to shame;
In dowie jyle they thocht his spunk to dern.

Creep back, ye scunnners – in ablow your stane.
You downa thole the licht o John Maclean
That rings abune – a mair nor Martian stern.

TO A NEW SOCIETY

It has been said that they cannot fathom my motive. For the full period of my active life I have been a teacher of economics to the working classes, and my contention has always been that capitalism is rotten to its foundations, and must give place to a new society. I had a lecture, the principal heading of which was 'Thou shalt not steal; thou shalt not kill', and I pointed out that as a consequence of the robbery that goes on in all civilised countries today, our respective countries have had to keep armies, and that inevitably our armies must clash together. On that and on other grounds, I consider capitalism the most infamous, bloody and evil system that mankind has ever witnessed. My language is regarded as extravagant language, but the events of the past four years have proved my contention.

He (the Lord Advocate) accused me of my motives. My motives are clean. My motives are genuine. If my motives were not clean and genuine, would I have made my statements while these shorthand reporters were present? I am out for the benefit of society, not for any individual human being, but I realise this, that justice and freedom can only be obtained when society is placed on a sound economic basis. That sound economic basis is wanting today, and hence the bloodshed we are having. I have not tried to get young men particularly. The young men have come to my meetings as well as the old men. I know quite well that in the reconstruction of society, the class interests of those who are on top will resist the change, and the only factor in society that can make for a clean sweep in society is the working class. Hence the class war. The whole history of society has proved that society moves forward as a consequence of an under-class overcoming the resistance of a class on top of them. So much for that.

[...] I wish no harm to any human being, but I, as one man, am going to exercise my freedom of speech. No human being on the face of the earth, no government is going to take from me my right to speak, my right to protest against wrong, my right to do everything that is for the benefit of mankind. I am not here, then, as the accused; I am here as the accuser of capitalism dripping with blood from head to foot.

– *John Maclean, Speech from the Dock, May 9th, 1918*

Freddie Anderson

BALLAD OF THE RED CLYDE

Come all ye Fake historians
and hiders of the Truth,
my story I will tell you,
and starting with my youth!
Beneath the mossy Lowther Hills,
my journey does begin,
on winding thro the Lanark Glades
and doon by Corra Linn.

I nurtured all those sylvan shades
where peasants tilled their fields,
and many a pleasant autumn hairst
those crops o' bounty yield:
on sun-lit streams and silver gleans,
I roam to wild and free
'til I join the tide
of the estuary wide
and dance into the sea.

I saw the Glasgow fishermen,
their little shielins build,
I saw the lairds deprive them
o' the very land they tilled;
I saw the poor gaunt weaving folk
all toiling night and day,
their weary sleep, their struggle deep,
their lives o' hodden grey.

I saw the Lanark miners
a similar fate endure,
the smelters doon by Waukenfield,
these legions of the poor,
and when they 'rose in protest deep,
to me 'twas no surprise,
for old clyde had seen, baith morn and e'en,
the anguish in their eyes.

The cruel bosses on my banks
no pity had nor shame;
with sword and gun at dead o' night
their hired troops all came,
and I wept to see such agony,
the sorrows and the loss
when they chained old 'Pearly' Wilson
and hanged him at the Cross.

I loaned my streams to Glasgow's poor,
my girth made deep and wide
'till I became in song and fame
the bonny river Clyde;
the riveters and caulker lads,
they sang in praise of me,
and waves that washed the anvilled yards
stirred yearnings to be free.

'Till there arose upon my banks
a stalwart breed of men,
who vowed that they would never be
poor suffering slaves again;

with dignity and courage stood,
nor did they stand in vain!
What joy to me to live to see
the likes of John Maclean.

Their emblem was the banner red,
they were no craven crew;
like Clyde has served you with its streams,
they lived and fought for you.
Their tribe still live throughout the years,
nor change with Time and Tide!
For liberty come sing with me
this ballad of the Clyde.

Archie Hind

SHOULDER TO SHOULDER *(extract)*

Bill: Hello it's you again.

Andy: Have you heard the news?

Bill: You mean about Kirkwood at Parkhead?

Andy: Aye. And about Jack Smith at Weirs.

Bill: Maxton and Jimmy McDougall.

Andy: Aye, I heard every last one o them's charged wi sedition.

Bill: Aye it's Butcher Haig and his yappin drover Lloyd George. It's mair men, mair men. Combing the country for mair men.

Andy: Mair bodies mair like.

Bill: Folk are weary o it. Weary o it. And the Glasgow Herald calls that weariness 'a vile conspiracy against the state.'

Andy: Bloody insult to injury. And this on top o them deporting the leaders o the worker's committee – McManus, Shields, Messer, Bridges, Glass. Aw deported.

Bill: Deported. Where?

Andy: Tae the wan place in Britain they can be sure they'll no start a revolution.

Bill: Eh?

Andy: Edinburgh.

(pause)

Bill: It's the Maclean trial they are worried about. They are trying to take away a his support.

Andy: Can they arrest the Clyde?

Bill: I'll be damned if they can.

Andy: Naw. Will you be there? For I'm goin myself.

Bill: Aye I'll be there. On the 11th April. I'll be in Queen Street. I'll be in the train wi the rest of them – and I'll take my fiddle and I'll play the Red Flag all the wey tae the high coort in Edinburgh.

Craig Smillie

MACLEAN TODAY

CHORUS:
Oh John Maclean, great John Maclean
We've need o you the night
When workin folk can tak nae merr
And stand up fur their rights
Tae ding they gallows doon
We huvtae find a way
Tae a warld o cooperation
Man, we need a Maclean the day

In the Great Glen o the Warld the day
Tyrants stalk the land
And leein politicians
Dish the dirt at their command
The vultures and the hoodies
Are croaking once again
The warld is ill-divided
We need you, John Maclean

In the dock you stated clear
How Freedom was fundamental
And you faced off they high heidyins
Lik Christ scourging the Temple
'I'm no here as the accused
I'm here as the accuser'
And you showed up their system
As the blood-drenched abuser

They gave ye penal servitude
In the jile at Peterheid
But the working class o Glesga
Demanded you be freed
They might have broke your body
But they couldna tear apart
Your Faith, your Love, your Vision
Your Passion and your Heart.

Amongst them a' ye tak yer stand
Liebknecht and Karl Marx
Mandela, Victor Jara,
Malcolm X and Rosa Parks,
Ghandi and Romero
Luther King and Sophie Scholl
 – Rise up wi' them and help us build
A warld that's fair for all

Alistair Hulett

DON'T SIGN UP FOR WAR

CHORUS:
He said a bayonet, that's a weapon wi' a working man at either end
Betray your country, serve your class. Don't sign up for war my friend
Don't sign up for war.

See thon Arthur Henderson, heid bummer o' the workin' men,
When war broke oot he pressed his suit an' ran tae catch the train
He signed a deal in London, nae mair strikes until the fightin's done
In Glesga toon the word went roon'. Tak tent o' John Maclean.

When they turned him oot o' Langside Hall, John stood up at the
    fountain
Whit he said was tailor-made tae magnify the friction
Ye patriots can roar and bawl, it's nought but braggarts fiction
The only war worth fightin' for is war against oppression.

The polis wheeched him oot o' there and doon tae Queens Park
    station
They telt him plain offend again an' we'll mak' ye rue the day, son
But Johnny didnae turn a hair, he ca'd for a demonstration
A mighty thrang ten thoosan strang turned oot against conscription.

The next time that they came for him, John kent they meant the
    business
He didnae plea for mercy, he said gi'e me British justice
The justice that he ca'd for stunned many intae silence
When oot o' hell the hammer fell, three years was the sentence.

The clamour tae release Maclean reached fever pitch and mair, man
In a year an a' hauf they ca'd it aff, but Christ it taxed him sair man
He came back auld afore his time, but he didnae seem tae care. Man
Dae a' ye can, I'm still the wan wha'll cause ye tae beware, man.

The last time that they jailed Maclean he came gey close tae scunnert
Wi' a rubber hose pit up his nose they kept him swap suppert
Let him oot or keep him in, Red Clyde was ower blaistert
Ilk wey they turnt the Government was weel and brawly gouthart.

Hamish Henderson

THE FREEDOM-COME-ALL-YE

Roch the wind in the clear day's dawin
Blaws the cloods heelster-gowdie ow'r the bay,
But there's mair nor a roch wind blawin
Through the great glen o' the warld the day.
It's a thocht that will gar oor rottans –
A' they rogues that gang gallus, fresh and gay –
Tak the road, and seek ither loanins
For their ill ploys, tae sport and play.

Nae mair will the bonnie callants
Mairch tae war when oor braggarts crousely craw,
Nor wee weans frae pit-heid and clachan
Mourn the ships sailin' doon the Broomielaw.
Broken faimlies in lands we've herriet,
Will curse Scotland the Brave nae mair, nae mair;
Black and white, ane til ither mairriet,
Mak the vile barracks o' their maisters bare.

So come all ye at hame wi' Freedom,
Never heed whit the hoodies croak for doom.
In your hoose a' the bairns o' Adam
Can find breid, barley-bree and painted room.
When Maclean meets wi's freens in Springburn
A' the roses and geans will turn tae bloom,
And a black boy frae yont Nyanga
Dings the fell gallows o' the burghers doon.

John McGrath, 7:84 Scotland

THE GAME'S A BOGEY *(extract)*

SONG: FREEDOM COME-ALL-YE

Bill: Internationalists first, last, and all the time.

(Dave comes forward with his guitar.)

Dave: Here's a song from Chile:

When I was a little boy
I went to work each day
No school for kids like me
No time to learn to play
Early every morning
They dragged me from my bed
I grew up tired and hungry
A worker like my dad.

Now I am a working man
I work in steel and wood
I'll tune an engine sweetly
Build houses true and good
One thing would be handy
You may think that I'm a fool
So much I'd like to learn
Hey, I wish I'd gone to school.

Now every man's a maker
A builder and a king

I make your roads and railways
I make you everything
I carve the earth with plough
Tunnel underground
I walk amongst the stars
And I make the world go round.

I learned to speak the words
My masters spoke so free
When I raised my voice
They came and murdered me
But they can't keep me down
As history has shown
A million hands will help me
For I am not alone.

(Dave leaves song unresolved, and speaks)

This song was written by a Chilean called Victor Jara. When the military overthrew and murdered Allende, he was one of many thousands arrested and taken to the football stadium in Santiago. Because he sang and played guitar for the prisoners, they broke the bones in both his hands. Because he still sang, they tortured him with electricity – he was in agony for two days and nights. And then they finished him off with sub-machine guns. He was just one of many thousands murdered by the Junta there. John Maclean died in 1923. This man, Victor Jara, died in 1973. 'I learned to speak the words my master spoke so free, but when I raised my voice they came and murdered me. But they can't keep me down, as history has shown, a million hands will help me, for I am not alone.'

THE BROKEN BODY AND UNBREAKABLE SPIRIT

Greetings to all comrades and the mass of the working-class who forced the Cabinet to release me! George Barnes's claim that he got my release is a lie as base as his betrayal of our class. He and the Cabinet members were really afraid for their very lives, and rightly so; for the workers have now reached a stage in the evolution of our class when they will punish their enemies in the great class war.

When leaving Peterhead, I told the governor, the head-warder, and others that if the workers made a bid for freedom along the lines of Russia and Germany, I would be in the thick of the fight, although aware that I would be the first to be captured by the real enemy, the propertied plunderers of Britain. Comrades can take it, then, that I am not 'tamed,' although the prison people did their utmost to accomplish the usual. The doctors this time made the most thorough test of my mind and character to find out such weaknesses as they might play upon in future to corrupt me into the betrayal of my class. It was beautifully done, but I can assure comrades that I beat the doctors at their game. I let them know that I was obsessed about nothing, not even life itself, and that they could burn all they thought they knew about me and have in tabulated and indexed form, as it would be of no use to them in my future fight against capitalism.

I have already received the greatest honour of my life in being appointed Scottish representative of the first Socialist Republic in the world, the Russian one; and the second, in being selected as the standard-bearer of my class by the Cabinet of the British capitalist class.

From a bread-and-butter point of view I don't need to sell out. I can go to Russia and be secure till I peg out. But I am not going to Russia, except on working-class business or for a holiday. The place for every British Socialist is here at home until capitalism is overthrown. I stay at home, then, with the Clyde Valley as my centre.

– *John Maclean,* The Call, *December 12th, 1918*

Dora Montefiore

TO JOHN MACLEAN TORTURED IN A CAPITALIST PRISON

Comrade right valiant with heart and with head
Comrade who always the Vanguard has led
Comrade your sufferings shall not be in vain!
Thousands are greeting you: 'Hail, John Maclean!'

Full well we know what you've done, what you've dared,
How all your actions with conscience are squared;
Now that we've heard of your torture and pain
Thousand will stand by you; 'Hail, John Maclean!'

Hark, through your prison bars thunders the call
'To hell with the torturers! Down with them all!'
Capital's power's at last on the wane!
Millions are helping you; 'Hail, John Maclean!'

Men such as Liebknecht and you are our need,
The People are rising; they ask for your lead;
They seek out the men of staunch heart and good brain,
They honour you... follow you... 'Hail, John Maclean!'

Hugh MacDiarmid

JOHN MACLEAN (1879–1923)

All the buildings in Glasgow are grey
With cruelty and meanness of spirit,
But once in a while one greyer than the rest
    A song shall merit
Since a miracle of true courage is seen
For a moment its walls between.

Look at it, you fools, with unseeing eyes
And denying it with lying lips!
But your craven bowels well know what it is
    And hasten to eclipse
In a cell, as black as the shut boards of the Book
You lie by, the light no coward can brook.

It is not the blue of heaven that colours
The blue jowels of your thugs of police,
And 'justice' may well do its filthy work
    Behind walls as filthy as these
And congratulate itself blindly and never know
The prisoner takes the light with him as he goes below.

Stand close, stand close, and block out the light
As long as you can, you ministers and lawyers,
Hulking brutes of police, fat bourgeoisie,
Sleek derma for congested guts – its fires
Will leap through you yet; already it is clear
Of all Maclean's foes not one was his peer.

As Pilate and the Roman soldiers to Christ
Were Law and Order to the finest Scot of his day,
One of the few true men in our sordid breed,
A flash of sun in a country all prison-grey.
Speak to others of Christian charity; I cry again
For vengeance on the murderers of John Maclean.

Let the light of truth in on the base pretence
Of Justice that sentenced him behind these grey walls.
All law is the contemptible fraud he declared it.
Like a lightning bolt at last the workers' wrath falls
On all such castles of cowards whether they be
Uniformed in ermine, or blue, or khaki.

Royal honours for murderers and fools! The 'fount of honour'
Is poisoned and spreads its corruption all through,
But Scotland will think yet of the broken body
And unbreakable spirit, Maclean, of you,
And you know you were indeed the true tower of its strength,
As your prison of its foul stupidity, at length.

John S Clarke

THE MAN IN PETERHEAD

When you've passed your resolutions,
>   When you feel you've 'done your bit,'
And you *think* there's nothing more that you can do,
>   Why not ACT – and in your action, try to emulate the grit
Of the Man in Peterhead who ACTS FOR YOU?

He is grateful for your money;
>   He appreciates your cheers;
And your sympathy is ample for his needs:
>   There are *more effective* things than resolutions, cash, or tears.
Why not give him just a sample, say – of DEEDS?

'Twas for you he garnered knowledge,
>   Sacrificed his very youth –
For you he worked until his head was gray.
>   They are killing him by inches just because he thought the
>   truth;
And having thought it, had the guts to SAY.

And the Truth's a kind of virtue
>   That the ruling classes fear:
By the foulest means to crush it they have tried.
>   For Truth, the stones of hate were hurled at prophet and at seer;
For Truth, the gentle Christ was crucified.

In a Rule Britannia prison
    John is rotting in a cell,
While Liebknecht from his fortress wanders free.
    Then remember, when for Freedom you are turning shot
    and shell,
There's a greater Freedom 'made in Germany.'

John was for the Revolution
    That will surely come in time,
For the sacred Flag of Liberty – the Red!
    That he bravely kept it flying was the burden of his 'crime,'
But he keeps it flying yet in Peterhead.

Will you suffer his destruction
    On the tyrant's battle-ground?
Will you let the cursed Wrong defeat the Right?
    He is One against an Army! – are you going to see him downed?
Are you going to let him die without a FIGHT?

He will pay you back in plenty,
    It is you who stand to gain;
For his Lion Heart is yours if he is spared.
    Then, toilers, for your own sakes UP AND LIBERATE MACLEAN.
You could DO IT – aye, tomorrow – IF YOU DARED!

Kay Ritchie

CONVICT NUMBER 2652

In Peterhead, Agnes found you force-fed,
half-dead on hunger strike and, like
Mahatma Gandhi or St Patrick or the suffragettes,
your fast, non-violent protest.

In catacomb-like Calton they dehumanised
by starving you of sustenance & social intercourse.
That silent cell. No sun. No snow. No stars.
Your daytime more like night.

And yet, Barlinnie let you write and read –
Einstein's relativity. Thomson's zoology.
Cunningham's industrial history.
Cohen's organic chemistry.

But in this penal prison, this Scottish gulag,
you, who'd fought for workers' rights,
fair rents, clean meat & peace,
were weakened by hard labour.

And like goose or duck being fattened for
the slaughter, foie gras for the rich man's table,
India rubber tubes invaded mouth &
slipped down gullet till you choked.

Feebled as those birds, coffin-cage-confined,
unable to stretch wing or fly to freedom,
you hungered for fresh air. Despaired.
And so did Agnes.

Uilleam Nèill (William Neill)

MOLADH IAIN RUAIDH

'Eil thu 'saoilsinn, aig a' cheann thall
gun do rinn e tabhartas gun bhuil?
gu robh grian mór ruadh a bheatha
a' dol fodha mu dheireadh air cuan marbh an eatorrais?
nach eil ar dùthaich mar a bha i –
na gleanntan farsuinn 's na srathan gun duine annta
ach ceannaichean coimheach 's an càirdean
a' marbhadh nan eun beaga an ainm spòrs,
fhad 's a tha mórshliochd Scota is Gaidheal Glas
gun aitreabh ach òtraichean breunach nam bailtean-móra?

A dh' ainneoin uile
tha sinne dìreach mar a bha sinn
'nar nàisean amaideach bhochd
fo stiùradh choigreach.

A dh' ainneoin uile
'sna làithean duaichnidh seo
is e sinne a tha am prìosan;
ach esan, fhad 's a mhaireas Alba
bidh feadhainn 'ga chuimhneachadh;
esan a tha saor gu sìorruidh
dìreach mar a bha e riamh.

Cò mise a bhith 'sgrìobhadh m' a dheidhinn
nach do dh' fhulaing na làithean dorcha
's a' phrìosan còmhla ris?

Cò thusa a chuireas clach
air càrn an duine seo?

IN PRAISE OF RED JOHN

Do you think, at the end of it all
that he made a useless offering?
that the great red sun of his life
went down at last on the dead sea of their mediocrity?
is our country not as it was –
the broad glens and the straths without a man in them
but alien hucksters and their friends
murdering the little birds in the name of sport,
while the great race of Scota and Gael Glas
are without a dwelling but the stinking dunghills of the cities?

In spite of all
we are just as we were
a poor foolish nation
under the control of strangers.

In spite of all
in these miserable days
it is we who are in prison;
but he, while Scotland lasts
some will remember him;
he who is free forever
just as he always was.

Who am I to be writing about him
who did not suffer the dark days
in the prison along with him?

Who are you who will put a stone
on the cairn of this man?

Sylvia Pankhurst

WRIT ON A COLD SLATE

Whilst many a poet to his love hath writ,
boasting that thus he gave immortal life,
my faithful lines upon inconstant slate,
destined to swift extinction reach not thee.

In other ages dungeons might be strange,
with ancient mouldiness their airs infect,
but kindly warders would the tablets bring,
so captives might their precious thoughts inscribing,
the treasures of the fruitful mind preserve,
and culling thus its flowers, postpone decay.

Only this age that loudly boasts Reform,
hath set its seal of vengeance 'gainst the mind,
decreeing nought in prison shall be writ,
save on cold slate, and swiftly washed away.

FELLOW CITIZENS, I COME BEFORE YOU

Fellow Citizens,

I come before you as the nominee of the Scottish Workers' Republican Party.

Today the wage-earning class is either partly or wholly idle and living on a starvation insurance or parish allowance, or fully employed at wages well below the 1913 level. Rotten food, under-supplies of food, insufficient clothing, overcrowding in sunless slums, loss of household goods to pawn-brokers, loss and reduction of pensions, worry over debts and the constant fear of eviction form the fate of a growing mass of workers. [...] Impoverished blood, disease, and death – that summarises the situation. The infant death-rate in Kingston in 1922 was 154, in Cathcart 28, i.e. eleven died in Kingston for every two in Cathcart.

The plight of the masses will be worse because of the European tangle of capitalist rivalries and political jealousies, hatreds and ambitions.

Capitalism is smashing itself to death in competition, strife, and bloodshed. In its path to destruction hundreds of millions of helpless people are being crushed by a growing poverty.

The clinging to capitalism, the ownership of the world by a small propertied class, is driving the people of this planet swiftly along the path to perdition.

The hope of humanity and the path to progress lies in the revolt of the wage-earners against the propertied class, the seizure of political power from the propertied class, and the seizure of the land and the means of production from the propertied class.

These seizures of political and economic power constitute the social revolution. The blood-shedding part of the business can safely be left to the Duke of Northumberland and his friends, the British Fascisti.

This great change means that the common people (the workers) will own the world in common, produce wealth in common, possess in common all wealth produced, and by common agreement distribute that wealth to the common advantage. This is a big task for the workers, but one forced on us by the worldwide misery of the masses. There is nothing frightful about the task. When this task is carried through the social stealing of class from class shall end for ever, and with the end of robbery armies and navies no longer shall be required, and social murder or warfare shall vanish for ever. This next form of human society is called communism.

Hence we put forward the following programme at this November election on the clear understanding that nothing we can do in the Town Council will materially alter the general condition of our class:

- Adequate compensation for the widow and children of Bernard Murdoch, murdered in the Southern Police Station.

- Release of Thomas Hitman at present lying in Barlinnie Prison under sentence of fifteen months for speaking for the unemployed.

- Prevention of evictions.

- Work for the unemployed, organised and executed by the Corporation at an adequate wage; or pressure on the government to provide an allowance adequate to maintain the unemployed.

- A roomy and well-equipped house for every family.

- Municipalisation of the milk, bread, clothing, and other supplies able to be handled by the Corporation.

- No work to be undertaken without the knowledge and consent of the employees' committees.

   – *Scottish Workers' Republican Party municipal election address, Used by John Maclean and all candidates in Glasgow, November 6th, 1923*

Nuala Watt

IMPORTANT INFORMATION ENCLOSED

We're ready to help get your bills down.
We're ready to break down your door
And gift you a pre-payment meter
To stop you from shivering more.

Perhaps you did not learn to budget,
But we can assist you with that.
And can we suggest, in the meantime,
You stay in one room in your flat?

We see you've restarted your asthma.
There's not enough gas for a bath.
You cough when you go to the bathroom.
A more parsimonious path

Could help you to quash all these problems.
And follow our energy plan.
We do understand, and we promise
To help you as much as we can.

Perhaps you could turn down your boiler.
Is your jacket too thin? Buy a spare.
The weather created this crisis.
We want you to know that we care.

Jim Ferguson

A REBEL LIFE

I.
Why are you not in the schoolbooks?

There's a statue and station stand in Dublin City
That tell of the British and how they shot Connolly
Here in Scotland his comrade, he lies unacclaimed,
For you are not in our schoolbooks brave John Maclean
Some folk now have barely heard of your fame
You are not in the schoolbooks bold John Maclean

II.
The Tramp's Trust unlimited

Sandy Ross, Peter Marshall
Young Harry McShane
James MacDougall & John Maclean,
consulates of new revolution

a story as auld as the bible
in the open air of Glasgow Green
in classrooms and in meeting rooms
on street corners and at factory gates

like wandering preachers
educate the workers
by every means:
a socialist college

a speech from the dock
a hunger march, an election campaign –

      a black and white photo
      on my grandfather's wall

      in Morgan Street, Govanhill,
      'Tramp Trust Unlimited'
      and my mother's voice:
      'Churchill was nuthin but a warmonger

      the best thing Glaswegian's ever done
      was protest against Churchill at Central Station'
      in 1951 that Tory gave a speech at Ibrox Park
      and warned against the dangers of socialism

      socialism gave us the NHS
      what does war bring?

Maclean is now ten decades gone
but still his message lingers on
bring us
      a Scotland Independent

bring us
      a Scottish Workers Republic

march into freedom,

          peace,

              and plenty.

III.
A politics of hope

earth
gives so
much

that
has been stolen
from us:

the greedy guards
their police
their bombs and guns
terrorise
our democratic
souls

and still
just look them in the eyes
and smile

they can never
rub us out

Election Ballad, 1918

MR JOHN MACLEAN, MP

(TUNE: *Private Michael Cassidy, VC*)

CHORUS:
John Maclean – he's come out of jail again –
    John Maclean – the Tyrant's enemy!
if you want to end the Workers' grief and pain,
    Make him Mr John Maclean, MP

Comrade John Maclean's the man we want to top the poll!
A fighter born and bred, he's in the fight with heart and soul.
So if you meet a man who seems to hesitate or doubt,
And don't know who to vote for, just go up to him and shout:

Thrice we've trusted Geordie Barnes, and found that we've
    been sold,
For when he went to Parliament he did what he was told;
But now we've got a man who dares the Master class oppose;
If you want to know his name, well, this is how it goes –

When the Factors started out to try their monkey tricks,
And threatened – if they got no rent – they'd surely pin our sticks!
Who was it told us, one and all, we should refuse to pay,
And got us organised, and led us on to victory?

The Coalition gang are out to promise us the earth:
But no we have heard that tale before and know what it is worth!
So now we're going to have the land, and give the boss the sack,
For Labour has arisen, and has found the man to back!

Thurso Berwick

SHOUT!

(TUNE: *Michael Row the Boat Ashore*. Election Song, 1967.)

CHORUS:
Shout to the man in Number 10 – Independence!
Scotland will be free again – Independence!

The River Tweed is a great divide – Independence!
Tak your stand on the Scottish side – Independence!

Good for the brown man, the black man too – Independence!
Good for me and good for you – Independence!

Now Wallace did not die in vain – Independence!
Neither did great John Maclean – Independence!

AC Clarke

JOHN MACLEAN'S THROAT

The megaphone through which he rallied crowds
against the armour-plated juggernaut
mowing them down in the name of progress,
against the barons of industry fattening on war;

the golden-tongued trumpet through which he sang
the truth of his cause, facing down judge and jury
with perfect pitch, not a flaw in his performance
winning the high ground though losing the battle;

the channel through which his keepers forced
humiliation: he would not swallow his words
so he must swallow their hard rations,
breaking his body though never his spirit;

the loudhailer still shouting itself hoarse
in the name of freedom, when in November chill
he stood coatless after his last reckless
act of charity, and was struck down.

Silenced forever the voice which had won over
thousands, whispered love-words to a wife,
declared for peace, spoken, in a fractured world,
for violence too, told stories to a daughter.

Kapil Seshasayee

SURROUNDED BY MY FRIENDS

It's easy to be hopeful
I cannot pretend
When I'm stood here by the plaza
Surrounded by my friends

IRISH STEW,

SCOTCH BROTH

Now the reaction is beginning – inspired by Ireland and Russia. Scotland must again have independence, but not to be ruled over by traitor chiefs and politicians. The communism of the clans must be re-established on a modern basis. (Bolshevism, to put it roughly, is but the modern expression of the communism of the mir.) Scotland must therefore work itself into a communism embracing the whole country as a unit. The country must have but one clan, as it were – a united people working in co-operation and co-operatively, using the wealth that is created.

We can safely say, then: back to communism and forward to communism.

The control must be in the hands of the workers only, male and female alike, each workshop and industry sending delegates to district councils and the National Council. The National Council must be based in or near Glasgow, as half the population lives within a radius of twenty miles from Glasgow.

In the period of transition a wage-earners dictatorship must guide production, and the adoption of the machinery and methods of production, to communist methods.

  – *John Maclean, All Hail the Scottish Communist Republic, August 1920*

Alan Bold

WORDS FOR JOHN MACLEAN

Scotland seems to happen in the past tense.
There is a swell of pride, a deep conviction
That sometime there was a land of innocence,
A land without a flaw whose facts and fiction
Were interchangeable and whose causes were just
In every case. There was murder at Flodden
And dear dead flowers who fell, there was that dust
That covered those who at Culloden
Left their blood to soak the bleak peat moor.
There was a prince whose Highland heart followed
His mind to thoughts of London, and a poor
Peasant who became a preacher and then swallowed
Half the seeds of Scotland's future. There was
A tenant-farmer who made a brilliant melody
And a fearless advocate who died so that the cause
Of the people should ultimately prevail, should finally
Triumph. And it has all happened, all been done,
Is all in our past, though not necessarily so.
There came from Pollokshaws a potter's son
Who frankly told old Scotland where to go.
And if we heed the deeds of John Maclean
Scotland will not be the same again.

George Hardie

SIC A LAND AS THIS

Whit manner o man was this?
For I, wha didna ken him,
can only caa him 'man'.
An yet, by aa accoonts, nae ordnar man.
Noble, wi that aristocracy o mind
that has nae need o pedigree or land
tae gie it lastin worth.
His was a vision. Bleezin,
bluid rid, across the firmament.
Owre bricht for lesser men tae watch.

(Whaur were they then, the people's fieres,
when he set aa the lift alowe?
Haudin their heids ablow the clathes
for fear their feeble sicht was tint!)

God! Was ever sic a land as this
whaur men o worth are cast
aside an auld dune sarks applauded?

Three heroes, worthy o the name, we've had
– an tint them aa!
Wallace, betrayed tae England's murderin croon,
Muir, banished tae a foreign shore,
an John Maclean. Deid frae a muckle dose
o great Britannic justice.

'A! Freedom is a noble thing!'
an scarce the Scot that's worthy o it.
Following fause prophets wha tint the wey
as suin as they set oot.
Buryin us aa, oot o the warld's kennin
happed in an Anglo Saxon shroud.

'The fault is nocht. I dar weel tak on hand
Nother in the people nor the land
As for the land it lackis na uther thing
Bot laubor and the pepyllis governyng.'
Oh! sic a land as this
that, in fower hunner year,
has yet tae learn that text.
Sir David Lyndsay syne Maclean
hae gien the ward an lit the flame
but still the vision is owre bricht
for purblin Scots tae seize.

Aye, even noo, their neypsie nebs
are coontin oot the cost
an playin Shylock
wi oor sovereign richts.

'Black be the day that e'er to England's ground
Scotland was eikit by the Union's bond.'
An blacker still the day
when balance sheets were taen tae be

the measure o a nation's richts.
God grant us grace,
an muckle grace we need,
that we maun yet contrive
tae heft this nation frae its knees,
keist faur its crutch
an, staunin straucht afore the warl,
lay claim tae whit's its ain.

No as a bankbuik
weel entered on the credit side,
but as a people
solven in oor ain identity.

Ruaraidh MacThòmais

ÀRMANN / WARRIOR

Fear de dh'àrmainn Mhuile is dòcha
ann a linn eile,
Iain Mac'IllEathain;
ach thilg eachdraidh do dhaoine
a chath ás ùr thu;
iolach a' Ghaidheil
a' tighinn á cliabh na Galldachd;
nam biodh seasmhachd as á lasair
sgrìobhte 'Saorsa' air nèamh Alba fhathast.

*   *   *

In another age
you might have been a 'warrior of Mull,'
John Maclean;
the history of your people flung you
into a new battle:
the Gael's exultant cry
coming from the chest of the Lowlands;
if only the flame lasted
it would write 'Freedom' on Scotland's sky yet.

Jim Aitken

CLEARANCES: A DIPTYCH

I.
Redemption

From Dornoch we moved further north,
not as north as where she was born
but north enough to understand;
to understand her returning.
She sat beneath the sculpture
of 'The Emigrants' at Helmsdale,
moved by the woman looking back
to the strath that was once her home.
For she too once had to leave here
to work in service or in shops;
she too, with some eighty years now,
lived in the south and not the north.
And these years have moved her to tears
and this woman brought them all back,
yet she sits with son and daughter
who marvel at her dignity.
Two highland ladies, one in bronze,
and the other in flesh that pains,
bestow upon a changing world
unchanging values that redeem.

II.
Clyde-Built

Once they threw us off our lands
made us sail the stormy seas
or scavenge along sea shores
beneath the tall dark cliffs
and still they made us fight their wars.

We came south in search of work
leaving the fresh smell of the heather
and the smell of burning peat
behind us as scents that had vanished
and still they made us fight their wars.

Maclean, McShane, Gallacher and Maxton
became our new clan chiefs, better than before
and we marched with them, our banners high
and the pipers played out at the front
as the Highlands and Lowlands combined.

Their legacy and the legacy of Davitt
came together too with Reid and Airlie
and Sammy Barr, as we worked on instead
showing a brand new kind of human dignity,
a Clyde-built face; built down all these ages.

And we need no memorial along these banks
because one exists already and stands proud
on the Clyde with her arms raised high
to the heavens. And we stood like La Pasionaria,
inspired by her, refusing to go on our knees.

Thurso Berwick

ANNI DOLENDI – DOMINO! (1923–1973)

for Nan Maclean Milton

They took the castles of his eyes
and gave them to the grim jailer.

And, as with Wallace,
they gave his singing to the five cold winds.

They drove a tunnel of progress
through the mountain of his head.

They laughed
and gave him to his friends
for burial.

His friends,
who took his right hand and chopped it off,
and said of him: He could not use it anyway.

His left hand they balled into a slogan
and hailed him for a hero.

And then
    in the dust of lies
    in the slag-hills of forgetfulness,
they buried their Conscience
    twice.

Anno dolories ... anni dolendi...
November gripping us,
and the Long Winter of fifty frozen years.
Then suddenly
the whirl of Fortune,
                    the shock of Destiny
flings up the burning sun

and in on the high season,
in from Rockall,
in through Eriboll,
in from the Islands,
in from the Forties
a jubilee of exaltation
                    bursts from the maverick seas.

anni dolendi – domino!

and swept in on a billion tons of oil,
swept into the command post,
singing,
        elemental,
                    red,
there stands again
the Permanence of Scotland,
the incorruptible Maclean.

David Morrisson

JOHN MACLEAN *(extract)*

General Election 1922
The banner of The Scottish Workers' Republican Party.
The first and last time?

30th November 1923,
John Maclean dead, aged 44.

This valiant fighter has not been forgotten. Next year a cairn
will be erected to his memory. Much of what he wrote is being
reprinted. This man, who died at the age of 44, gave all he
had to give for the cause he believed in.
  – Harry McShane, 'Remembering John Maclean', *New*
    Edinburgh Review, Number 19, 1972

November 1972, I sit and write of this man,
The rebel, clean cut and true,
But the crux of history, does it make him
Like MacDiarmid now, almost respectable,
A great man, but yet another crank to
            Scotland's cause?

Good for the academic indulging in ideas,
Sitting in his dusty cell.
Good to have cocktail-debate about
how Clydeside, Scotland might have gone.

(Old age and death are easy to handle.)

Ay, it's so easy to deal with ideas
From the distance of time and place;
It's so easy for us to make pleas,
Memory against the Capitalist race.

It's so easy, or yet is it the case
That Maclean, MacDiarmid have given words
To what the mass truly believe.

It is that they had courage
When it was easier, more comfortable for us
To be cowards in a cowardly place.

It's so easy to join the ranks
        of mass complacency;
It's so easy to believe in the great crank
        – voice of your spirit –
But keep him well from the public eye.
A few against the mass, you cannot deny
        it's a cause doomed to fail.

At the right time, the right place
        you could swell the ranks, oh yes.

Was there a right time, a right place
        for MacDiarmid, for Maclean?

Nisha Ramayya

ANENT PRECENTING THE LINE

*   *   *

             'LET US SUFFICE
TO SAY THAT IT IS THE SURVIVOR
OF THIS TALE THAT HANGS OUT
HER STORY TO DRY ON THE
WASHING LINE OF REMEMORY'

in surviving she gives out the line
that a chorus might be drawn as these
subjects are to more heat than light

in giving she tunes the repetition
unbleached dresses still dripping trade
winds knotted with workers' songs

in telling she coruscates the web
lapses flash to do undid interactions
syrcas restores the bending touch

*   *   *

what those great men gave up on behalf of their children
to find fortune in graves, to propagate unnatural names

leveraging their inheritance: *don't just subsist by learning,*
strew the clearing with the bright lights of benevolence

rivers like biomimetic circuitry of extraction
                    'shipping routes spread out from Glasgow
                                        like the ribs of a fan'

enlightened bystanders are on hand taking questions on looting
as red-cloaked nation strides past, the inevitability
                    of his gold-tipped cane, proselytised

*   *   *

attending to the story that is mystified yet
totalising at the expense of counter-nations:

'the nation' (to which, of course, the people
who have been "converted" do not belong)'

children must give thanks for being sacrificed
the profits of their destitution sight unseen

the story that might be better known yet
under-studied, the city teaches us to look

up

*   *   *

this city, where the millionaire capital passes the murder capital
in the street, nods without smiling at its own reflection, clutches
its purse, the matrix of chicken tikka masala's self-renunciation,
conveying the fancy for imperial rule, sows' ears made from tar

*   *   *

– following a line down Albert Drive – where cultural contact springs up like forests – marking the spots that require unearthing – ornament is grafted on the hardy and resolute – pinky, pista, and jalebi sticky the tramway tracks with Glasgow's other colours – whilst fair-weather temperaments construct themselves as foreign for mutual reward – at every strata in the terms of the rich – crossing Shields Road towards Victorian mansions built strong enough to hold ceilidhs in the attic, so say letters sent back home – admiring this nominal relationship to the flower and whispering to find out what old-new complicities it tends – if the 'noble passion' is free to claim or denounce – insofar as nobility is limitless when sequestered from power there is a jaw parallel to the ground – defensive posture compromised as the nasal cavity is exposed, a midge might dart in or a more sinister fleck – cryptozoological beasts do more than line their nests with tartan – men who were moved moved to move other men, another outline that distracts from the matter – through the ghosts of cotton mills in Pollokshaws, martyrdom's composers – all echoes might be seeded with fractal paisleys – unravelling in a manner diametrically opposed to Draupadī's sari, that is, unravelling – like the beloved juxtapositions that adumbrate violence and disavow reparations in the eyes of liberals – but roots move differently, sound out reckoning's blur, fathomless causes and effects beyond geometry's key to history – 'I am not here, then, as the accused; I am here as the accuser of capitalism dripping with blood from head to foot' – cheery and dangerous, or cheery because dangerous, a Scottish link in the golden chain of world socialism – a mile and a half from where I grew up, feels closer today –

*   *   *

When Hortense Spillers says: 'I'm wondering if the whole society didn't escape, if abuse became the order of the day', we must stop what we're doing and down our critical tools; her remark is our event is the world's gravitational field. Without thinking about it, thus letting go of it, we might try to feel what it means, with and without touching, with and without the capacity and liability of being touched. Invoke the vertical plane to confine the inquiry to tobacco lords and their sons, or forsaken clanspeople and evictees, or planters, or soldiers, or inheritors of the ancient universities, accountants, doctors, clerics...; notice how these images reflect and contort according to what holds up the mirror and who stands before it, how the question of a nation's truth can limit the reach of its answers; extinguish the wall with the supreme understanding that walls are not found in nature, which is this inquiry's unconfinability, a spiralling formulation that allows us to sustain the project thanks to regular stoppages and explosions.

*   *   *

'But enough about me. How have you been doing?

I know you only exist
when called upon, and the call is not voluntary
but takes the place of an obscenity
and does not even contain your name.' – Peter Manson

does not ev en con tain your name
does not ev en con tain
the mat ter of your name in sound
in sound as in rest less

ness as in res pon ding with warmth
if your name could give out
like song in flight to the tem ple
of truth vib rat ions seats

flocks re turn black en ed sound ing
the het er o phon ic
range of your names ex is tence can't
con tain your be com ing

> 'We return full circle back to the blues, back to "the
> Internationale", back to forms of anti-capitalist resist-
> ance that extend beyond an industrial proletariat, back
> to visions of freedom [...] and a willingness to confront
> the present with revolutionary pessimism even if mixed
> with anticipatory optimism [...] If you could make "the
> Internationale" into the blues it would be pessimism
> and joy, and it would be a text you'd keep writing on and
> writing on and writing on...' – Robin DG Kelley

> this song a text you'd keep writ ing
> on this cir cle a cy
> mat ic de mand to fol low each
> line to the ends of time

> to their buds you'd go be yond work
> be yond sub ju ga tion's
> false friend ship hills col lapse in to
> red cent re burn ing dock

buds bridge bridg es sing back your steps
you don't go pre vi ous
you go tubes with in tubes pull through
and min gle free dom clues

> 'The communism of the clans must be re-established
> on a modern basis [...] [Scotland] must have but one
> clan, as it were – a united people working in co-
> operation and co-operatively, using the wealth that
> is created.
>
> We can safely say, then: back to communism and
> forward to communism.' – John Maclean

we can say back we can say for
wards our say ing bodi ies
green skies milk strike ma ny good arms
un cross en tranced stretch time

our nat ur al names spo ken with
love dis perse side real ly
call back to earth worms groove soc ial
life through out un i verse

> 'The volute, you see, is divine: the sinuous
> line, the serpentine line, the corolla, the curl,
> the twist, the whorl, the spiral and so on,
> are all related in their volution, convolution,
> revolution. Volution is the essential and
> irreducible aspect of ornamentation, just as
> the phoneme is the smallest irreducible unit
> of sound in language.'
> – Erskine-Lily / Shola von Reinhold

ir red uc ib le div ine line
for got ten race ri ots
re al co op er a tion cho
rus of can't take it do

    'that echo and lesson of the blues' – Arjuna
    Neuman and Denise Ferreira da Silva

    ech o les son in ten der ness

*   *   *

1. Sulter, M. (2015) 'A Brief Introduction', *Maud Sulter: Passion*, ed.
   Deborah Cherry (Altitude Editions), p. 7a.
2. Ian Charles Cargill Graham cited in Devine, T. M. (2004) S*cotland's
   Empire: The Origins of the Global Diaspora* (London: Penguin Books),
   p. 72.
3. Marx, K. (1990) 'The Expropriation of the Agricultural Population',
   Capital Volume I, trans. Ben Fowkes (London: Penguin Books), p. 888.
4. John Maclean cited in Bell, H. (2018) *John Maclean: Hero of Red
   Clydeside* (London: Pluto Press), p. 107.
5. Hortense Spillers interviewed by Arjuna Neuman and Denise Ferreira
   da Silva (20th March 2020). [My transcription.]
6. Manson, P. (2016) 'Time comes for you', *Factitious Airs* (Glasgow: Zarf
   Editions), p. 12.
7. Kelley, R. D. G. 'Internationale Blues: Revolutionary Pessimism and
   the Politics of Solidarity', LSE Public Lectures and Events (17th May
   2019). [My transcription.]
8. John Maclean cited in Bell, *John Maclean*, p. 160.
9. Shola von Reinhold, *Lote* (London: Jacaranda, 2020), p. 310.
10. Neuman, A. and Ferreira da Silva, D. (2021) *Soot Breath // Corpus
    Infinitum*.

THE BIRTHDAY OF THE NEW WORLD

[...] old friends were embracing, laughing, all talking at once. A lesser man might have joined his colleagues beside the samovar, but Lenin did not linger in the midst of the melee. Instead, he found his way upstairs and out on to the balcony.

It was the only place in the main building that was visible to passers-by beyond the garden walls. Kshesinskaya's nearest neighbour, just a silhouette of dark on dark at this late hour, was the Petrograd mosque, and all around was open space with ghostly, leafless parkland trees. Leaning into the night, Lenin could sense the perfect opportunity to make a speech. 'Germany is in ferment,' he told the small crowd that still lingered in the shadows below. In Britain, he bellowed, the anti-war agitator John Maclean had been imprisoned. The names and details might have been a little alien to Russian ears, but the news was thrilling and the speaker's hoarse but raging tone entirely original. It was only when Lenin began to rail against the capitalist war that the atmosphere stated to curdle. 'Ought to stick our bayonets into a fellow like that,' a soldier shouted, 'Must be a German.'

– Lenin on the Train, *Catherine Merridale, (New York: Metropolitan Books / Henry Holt and Company, 2017), pp.222 - 223*

6–7 November 1917 will ever be celebrated as the dawn o the wage-slaves' freedom – the birthday of the new world rising out of the ruins of the old society of robbery, tyranny, and universal murder. The down-trodden workers and peasants of Russia responded to the call of the Communist Manifesto of 1848, by uniting on that day and expropriating the landlords and capitalists of the Russian empire; and despite the concentrated attack of world capitalism they may hold out long enough to allow of the rest of the working class responding to the same old call: 'Workers of the World, Unite!'

– *'On with the revolution!', John Maclean,* The Call, *6 November 1919*

Maclean is in prison because he came out openly as the representative of our government, but we have never seen this man, he has never belonged to our Party, he is the beloved leader of the Scottish workers, but we joined with him the Russian and Scottish workers united against the British government...

– *Concluding Speech at 4th Congress of Trades Unions, V. I. Lenin, June 29th, 1918*

Hugh MacDiarmid

THE KRASSIVY POEM

Scotland has had few men whose names
Matter – or should matter – to intelligent people,
But of these Maclean, next to Burns, was the greatest
And it should be said of him, with every Scotsman and Scotswoman
To the end of time, as it was of Lenin in Russia
When you might talk to a woman who had been
A young girl in 1917 and find
That the name of Stalin lit no fires,
But when you asked her if she had seen Lenin
Her eyes lighted up and her reply
Was the Russian word which means
Both beautiful and red.
Lenin, she said, was 'krassivy, krassivy'.
John Maclean too was 'krassivy, krassivy',
A description no other Scot has ever deserved.

Edwin Morgan

ON JOHN MACLEAN

'I am not prepared to let Moscow dictate to Glasgow.'
Failures may be interesting, but it is the firmness
of what he wanted and did not want
that raises eyebrows: when does the quixotic
begin to gel, begin to impress, at what point
of naked surprise?
                              'I for one will not follow
a policy dictated by Lenin until he knows
the situation more clearly.'
                              Which Lenin hadn't time to,
and parties never did – the rock of nations
like the rock of ages, saw-toothed, half-submerged,
a cranky sputtering lighthouse somewhere, as often
out as lit, a wreck of ships all round,
there's the old barnacled 'Working-class Solidarity,'
and 'International Brotherhood' ripped open and awash,
while you can see the sleekit 'Great-Power Chauvinism'
steaming cannily past on the horizon
as if she had never heard of *cuius regio.*
Maclean wanted neither the maimed ships
nor the paradox of not wanting them
while he painfully trimmed the lighthouse lamp
to let them know that Scotland was not Britain
and writs of captains on the Thames
would never run in grey Clyde waters.

Well, nothing's permanent. It's true he lost –
a voice silenced in November fog. Party
is where he failed, for he believed in people,
not in *partiinost* that as everyone knows
delivers the goods. Does it? Of course.
And if they're damaged in transit you make do?
You do – and don't be so naive about this world!
Maclean was not naive, but
'We are out
for life and all that life can give us,'
was what he said, that's what he said.

Alisdair Gray

POOR THINGS *(extract)*

after Archie Hind

John was not a Zapata, galloping on horseback over the corn-fields. He was of the peasantry who fed Zapata. He was not a Lenin, working to move his office into the Kremlin. He was of the Kronstadt sailors whose mutiny gave Lenin the chance. John was not the sort who lead revolutions. He was the sort who make them.

Alec Finlay

AFTER SPICER AFTER LORCA

a green boat
in blue water

and a beautiful
black fish

a blue boat
in green water

and a lovely
white oyster

a red boat
on a red river

and a shared
shoal of silver

Alistair Mackie

THE DARG O JOHN MACLEAN

I mind on the speech o Pasternak
at the First Writers' Congress –
he wanted, he said, to lift
fae the shouthers o the workin quine in the Metro
the wecht o her wark-loom,
and that as o a sudden, she
was a sister to him
and he wanted to help her
as gin she'd been an auld an dear frien.

           You
did mair nor want, John Maclean;
ye socht an focht to lift
fae aff the shouthers o working fowk
the Atlas wecht o centuries,
the doon-drag an trauchle
that gart the warld birl
iled by the bleed o men.

A thocht yon;
to heist the yirth fae its aixle-tree
till the back-bane could staund up straucht
and caa itsel – a man.
Naething less nor that, and that
but a pint on the rim o aathing
ye lived and deid for.

Nou fiftie year efter the yirth took ye in
Scotland still stands it seems
a Winter Palace o the spirit,
and your time-boomb – a whuff o Lenin's breath –
ticks on aneath that wecht.

Oor poems are rhetoric
to your life and death –
the future conscience o the yirth.

Nuala Watt

JOHN MACLEAN, 'QUAKER'

*The only way to end all the trouble is by the establishment of
socialism – (Christ having failed)*

I would know. You would be a favourite Quaker story, like Fox
or Penn or Fell. We would argue in the John Maclean Room and
mend the roof from your memorial fund. I checked the books
of members and attenders. Barlinnie got it wrong. You weren't
a Friend.

I see the warder rushing through religions. *Well, he must be something on this list.* It makes a sort of hurried prison sense – and you
were objecting to conscription. 'Quaker' as prison shorthand for
conundrum. Puzzling zealot. Does not go to church.

Prison is a favourite Quaker story. I trust your sufferings in
Peterhead more than Dewsbury's euphoria – *I joyfully entered
prisons as palaces* he wrote, but only after he was free.

You followed Christ the activist, then stopped. Would you have
trusted us – still in our wealthy shoes and chocolate phase?
Did Rowntree's, Clarks or Barclay's ever strike? Still – as Penn
said – *true godliness don't turn men out of the world but enables
them to live better in it and excites their endeavours to mend it* so
perhaps.

I suspect you were awkward as Fox – desperate to turn the world over. If you weren't, it's a *silly poor gospel* to leave your little girls.

*   *   *

Quotations from John Maclean, 1915; William Dewsbury, 1688; William Penn, 1682; Margaret Fell, 1700 in Quaker Faith and Practice (Britain Yearly Meeting of the Religious Society of Friends)

Alan Riach

THE LINE OF JOHN MACLEAN

Tarzan in the pond at Dublin Zoo, in 1928,
With Erskine, Grieve & Yeats all looking on –
Grieve is thinking of Maclean, as the water music splashes
On his shoes. Erskine is saddening, time is swimming away.
Yeats watches that slim body, muscular, fast-moving,
White as a fish in the liquid element: darting straight,
Weissmüller young, eight years before the first film starts:
All under the eye, benevolent, permissive, of good Queen Tailte,
Who cleared the fields for future's harvests: these, her games,
The Scots, the guests; the Irish, hosts, hosting heroes.
All hail the approaching Workers' Republic of Scotland!
Maclean proclaimed, after talking with Erskine of Marr.
Hail, neighbours! That sharp perceptive twist, in 1920,
That was MacLean. And then MacDiarmid, 1938, affirms it
In and as 'The Voice of Scotland': *The Line of John MacLean.*
It takes some time to see exactly what a straight line is,
In all the sharp distortions of the water, broken
Up like splinters, flakes and shards of mirror, glass,
Its razor edges dangerous, cutting flesh, and misdirecting vision.
But this one thing comes through, clean and clear and travelling fast,
In one direction only, like Tarzan through that Dublin pond, back then,
To now, and here, and on: the further destination, thus defined.

NOTE: C.M. Grieve or Hugh MacDiarmid and Ruaraidh Erskine of Marr were among the guests at the Tailteann Games in Dublin in 1928. At the inaugural Games in 1924, W.B. Yeats also attended, and the 24-year old Olympic swimmer and Tarzan-to-be Johnny Weissmüller, swam the pond at Dublin Zoo. Whether the writers saw him, I don't know, and in the poem I've conflated the events, but John MacLean's meeting with Erskine in Glasgow on 21 July 1920 seems almost certainly to have prompted MacLean's pamphlet All Hail the Scottish Workers' Republic! *of August that year, establishing his move from 'British' socialism to Scottish Republicanism, and MacDiarmid invokes this proposition explicitly in the first essay of the first issue of his journal* The Voice of Scotland *(Vol.1, No.1, June-August 1938, although he had already drawn it up in 1936): 'The Red Scotland Thesis: Forward to the John MacLean Line'. Tailte was the Celtic deity who cleared the fields of Ireland for future cultivation. She exhausted herself and died as a result. You could say MacLean too was taking part in a similar struggle, as were Erskine of Marr and MacDiarmid: they knew the pathos of the epic effort.*

Robert Kiely

LESSONS

there are things in the history
          windtunnel
there's no transition in the fossil record
the soft bits don't get preserved
  there's some things
    in the dark
    and history cannot overcome them

*   *   *

the society of missed boats
under permanent siege

*   *   *

money has mouths but says nothing
and
there's a speech
and all possible histories cannot overcome it

*   *   *

you see saws and shells
the soft bits don't get preserved
they don't have to
preservation is for the sales and transport departments
they don't send in paramilitaries
they don't have to the soft bits reading groups workshops

*   *   *

spit out the hard bits
there's something in the dark
the darkness cannot overcome it

*   *   *

this unforgiveable sky

INTERNATIONALISTS

FIRST, LAST

AND ALL THE TIME

The only atonement Britain can make for the slaughter and injury of perhaps more than three thousand people at Amritsar is self-determination for India. It is very cunning to give a report of the Amritsar massacre more than a year after the bloody deed, dismiss the murderer, General Dyer, and then discuss him in the House of Thieves. The Thieves have confirmed his dismissal (with a very fat pension and probably secret gifts galore for 'saving India') and expect the world to believe that this compensates for the cold-blooded massacre. It won't do. The only reparation is independence for India, and nothing less...

  – *'Up, India!', John Maclean,* The Vanguard, *August 1920*

The government seized the occasion afforded by the miners' strike to let the hunger-striker Fitzgerald die in Cork prison. Now Lord Mayor MacSwiney has been killed in Brixton Prison after a torture of seventy-four days [...] Comrades, champion Ireland's cause with trebled energy and thus avenge the martyred Lord Mayor. Never in all our reading of history have we read of a slower and more cruel torture than that practised in Brixton Prison [...] Down with the bloody government that attempts to do such deeds in our name! Down with the system of greedy capitalism that develops blood-mania on its dominant classes!

  – *'Stray straws', John Maclean,* The Vanguard, *November 1920*

Claude McKay

IF WE MUST DIE

If we must die, let it not be like hogs
Hunted and penned in an inglorious spot,
While round us bark the mad and hungry dogs,
Making their mock at our accursèd lot.
If we must die, O let us nobly die,
So that our precious blood may not be shed
In vain; then even the monsters we defy
Shall be constrained to honor us though dead!
O kinsmen! we must meet the common foe!
Though far outnumbered let us show us brave,
And for their thousand blows deal one death-blow!
What though before us lies the open grave?
Like men we'll face the murderous, cowardly pack,
Pressed to the wall, dying, but fighting back!

Victoria McNulty

FROM HEAD TO FOOT

No government is going to take from me my right to speak, my right to protest
against wrong, my right to do everything that is for the benefit of mankind.
– John Maclean

The bones in our press are a floating fire hazard
A bog buried shame
Regurgitated at a port in Dorset
The flesh of our sins swings in sculleries
Pulley-drawn names
Misspelled in the wind between Govan and Sarajevo
On your centenary Glasgow Life lit a red rag
Hoist it above a driving range
A quaint serenade to pension paid drones and cluster bombs
Christ John, if you were around to see them
take your name in vain
You'd rise from the page
An accuser again.

In 2019 local authority pensions in Glasgow were linked to the funding of
weapons complicit in war crimes in Yemen. That same year, the city celebrated
the centenary of Red Clydeside and the leadership of John Maclean.

Jackie Kay

WHEN PAUL ROBESON CAME BACK TO GLASGOW

*He lived in our times, we live in his... It is a matter of bearing witness
to that force which moved among us.* – James Baldwin

When Paul Robeson came to Glasgow,
our cherry tree was just a pip.

I wasn't born, but they had our Maxie
and they lived at Brackenbrae, 183.

That day, the first of May 1960,
Gary Frances Powers was shot down flying U-2,

a prisoner was gassed to death in the USA
at precisely 10.02

and people from both sides of the Atlantic
were singing Elvis Presley's 'Stuck on You'.

It was a warm, sunny day,
Sunday in the Park with Paul!

Everybody, even the weans, walking tall,
everybody having a ball with Paul!

And it seemed the whole o' Glesca Toon
opened its arms to the man:

*My people, my people
Body and soul*

And what is Glasgow if not a place of welcome
to the citizens of the world:

the Nelson Mandelas, the Madame Allendes,
    the Paul Robesons?

*   *   *

He'd come to lead the May Day Parade
and he marched from George Square;

with the women pipers, the postal workers,
the brass bands, the Clydeside Apprentice Committee.

And the dear green welcomed him,
a city embrace to a giant of grace, Paul Robeson...

In his good coat, raising his hat, politely,
in thanks for the gift of the city keys.

Down Jamaica Street and across the Clyde.
Down the Broomielaw, Paul in his prime.

No return to the Hungry Thirties
left then right and up Victoria Road

where Pat Milligan used to bide.
And it was Paul, Paul who led the way.

The man who came from Robeson County
whose father was a slave who worked the tobacco fields,

the man who played Othello,
who had *that deep bass voice,* who played baseball

and sang spirituals as well as Bach or Handel,
who loved the Hebridean songs,

the pentatonic mode, whose voice soared to Eriskay,
to the river Jordan; *Volga Volga.*

Who brought Joe Hill back, sang 'Ho-ri Ho-ro',
taught himself Gaelic and German, Paul all the way

in the city of the word, past Queen's Park Café,
the bird that never flew, the fish that never swam,

where great John Maclean came home from the Clyde,
Paul, with his compañeros side by side.

Shoulder to shoulder, with the miners, weavers,
the joiny inners, ghosts of comrades in the May air.

And all the banners raised
Playing Fields Not Battle Fields

alongside the Socialist Sunday school,
and they sang

I'm going to lay down my sword and shield
Down by the riverside. Paul

who had known rivers, ancient dusky rivers
whose soul had grown deep like the rivers,

Paul, whose passport was taken from him –
Un-American Activities, so called – Paul

who had a calling, who answered the response
with a call, who walked among us that day

to Queen's Park and got up on that stage
to a roar of love 10,000 strong. Paul, Saul-Saul

who had *a balm in Gilead to make the wounded whole,*
to heal the sin-sick soul, Paul

who knew the struggle of any people
cannot be by itself, who fought for his own.

When he spoke that day in Queen's Park
he said, *It is as if I have come home.*

*   *   *

His soul has grown deep in rivers
In the Jordan Creek, in the Hudson River Basin
In the Shoe Heel Creek, in the Goodman Swamp
In the Hackensack River, in the Little Raft Swamp
In the Lumber River, in the Raritan River
In the Thames, in the Wye, in the Dee, in the Clyde
In the Old Man's River, where one river meets another.

*   *   *

Let Robeson sing his song.
Been lonesome for too long.
Had no sun deep in the river bed
amongst the reeds, minnows, perch, carp –
the man who once played on track is coming back.

Anyone who has graced Glasgow
owns Glasgow's grace.

I dreamed I saw Paul Robeson last night
alive as he could be, alive alive oh.

*   *   *

My mother once said, without a hint of irony –
but doing the ironing – *If I hadnae married your father,
I'd have gone for Paul Robeson.*

She lost her job back in 1956
campaigning for the return of Robeson's passport.
Let Robeson sing

*He must know something
but he don't say nothing*

And when Paul Robeson comes back to Glasgow today
the city once again opens its wide arms

and George Square fills with red mist.
And Douglas dances and Suzanne sings

and the city that had seen all manners
of tragedy and triumph lifts itself up again.

When Paul Robeson walks down from the east to the west
with Rabbie at his back and the Chamber's big YES –
all the struggles come together as one.

But I ain't dead, says he.
But I ain't dead, says he.

Mary Brooksbank

THE ROAD

Were I tae tell a' the things that I ken,
Ye'd say I wis daft.
So I'll jist haud my pen,
For I know that time's passing
Will surely show
The road they're a' feared at
Is the road we maun go.

Fae the lips o' lang deid but remembered men,
Burns, Muir and Lenin, our ain John Maclean,
Liebknecht and Rosa, wi' voice and wi' pen,
What telt us ower and ower again,
Urging us forward, whit maks us sae slow
While they block wi' their atom
The road we maun go.

Juana Adcock

AN AK-47 IS A WEAPON WITH WORKERS ALL AROUND IT

My blood revolts against... brutally blatant capitalism in America, a capitalism that means to crush Mexico under its 'heel of steel' – John Maclean

An AK-47 is a weapon with workers all around it
workers striking over pay in the factory that produced it
workers dying of thirst all along the sun-beaten geographies
    of export
and transport of weapons and workers across borders
workers in police uniform using weapons to abuse workers
workers around the world whose grandparents (like Maclean's)
    were forced from their land
into a life of servitude to make way for cattle
workers forgetting their mother tongues
workers in the city whose bosses do not speak their mother tongues
workers living in crowded conditions, health impaired from
    poor diet
workers with minds trapped, driven to anger and addiction
workers driving the economy of the arms exporting nations
and the economies of the global south booming in a state of fear,
    violence, and impunity
workers with Mexican drug cartels firing American or German
    .50 calibre bullets
tearing through buildings, helicopters, and tanks
workers caught in the crossfire between their own armed groups,
    armies, police forces.

The bosses' heel of steel on the chest
and their hands on the throat of indigenous workers everywhere
their knee on the neck and their hands on the head of workers
and I do not ask them for mercy (says Maclean).
I am not here to ask for mercy, I am here to fight.

Lola Olufemi

STRIKE!

What's the mood of the general strike? I think something changes in the air. Particles rearrange themselves to spell enough kidnapping in the dead of night, murder, endless poverty stretching for miles and miles. If you observe the mood, you might be able to hear your heartbeat in your tooth and then your toenail, then the very tips of your fingers. The mood of the general strike is not in the body of man. It's burrowed deep in the earth; it begins to shake every time the past defeats itself and the clock simmers. The mood of the general strike might only be defined by what it is not. If I had to approximate, I can only say something like, imagine if you are a free diver and you break the surface when you were expecting to drown. Imagine that breath: the sheer scope of it, the relief that floods through you. In Haiti and Sudan, it's hot sun and barricading the streets. For Amazon workers in America, it's union meetings in non-descript buildings; for the enslaved it was choosing your own death, sabotaging commodity. The general strike happens when North meets South. It's when newness runs its fingers over the impasse that is the contemporary. The general strike is a point of departure; it's strike-out, a refusal to play the game, it's a strike, the act of marking one's target; it's a strike, an act of violent insurrection, it's a strike, a correction of the old mistake, it's a strike, hard to read and even harder to describe. The mood of the general strike is... solemn. It's the moment you realise that you have to do something with the life you have taken back.

The general mood of the general strike is the parcelling out of the bosses' bones to pick our teeth with. The mood of the general strike is either you are with us or you will be crushed, no nuance. The mood of the general strike is scorched earth and nobody narrating as it happens. The mood of the general strike is when the text becomes discernible, just for a moment. The general strike is staring at what was once obscured until you can make out its edges, like you are doing now. It's recognition despite restriction. A recognition of yourself for what you are: a worker. The general strike says: instead of working for the man, let's work for love, let's work for each other, let's work for song and for dance, let's work in service of pleasure. Let's work and work and work so finally we can talk about something other than work.

What's the colour of the general strike? Well, to know that, you have to know the colour of the future, that's easy. A mix of every colour currently imaginable, but mostly that colour is the absence of light. You know the one.

Somhairle MacGill-Eain (Sorley MacLean)

AN CUILITHION *(às-earrann)*

Mòr am blàr is na creuchdan
tha an èirig na h-Eòrpa;
cruaidh an gleac iomagain
tha an tuigse na còrach;
cian fada 'n imcheist
is iomaluas na breòiteachd,
fada 'n oidhche 's a h-iargain
mun tig grian dhearg òraidh.

Fada, ach thig i,
's ann dhuinn thig an òr-ghrian;
èiridh an Cuilithionn
gu suilbhir 'na ghlòir geal;
ged as searbh dhuinn an oidhche
chuir an loinneas fo sgleò dubh,
's ann a bhristeas a' mhadainn
air baidealan glòrmhor.

Cruaidh càs na Sìne,
nan Innsean 's na h-Albann,
searbh call na Spàinne,
àrainn nam mòr mharbh;
cruaidh càs na h-Eadailt,
na Gearmailt 's na Frainge,
is uachdarain Shasainn
a' cur am bochdan fo ghanntachd.

Tha Ó Conghaile an Èirinn
ag èirigh thar àmhghair,
MacGill-Eain an Albainn
'na chalbh air na h-àirdean,
Liebknecht sa Ghearmailt
marbh ach neo-bhàsmhor,
is Lenin an Ruisia,
ceann-uidhe nan sàr-bhreith.

THE CUILLIN *(extract)*

Great the war and wounded blood
that is the ransom of Europe;
hard the agony wrestling,
in the realisation of Justice;
long, long the perplexity
and the manifold wretchedness,
long the night of longing
before the red-gold sun comes.

Long, but come it will,
the gold sun will come to us;
The Cuillin will rise
affable in his white glory;
bitter the night to us
that put your beauty under a dark shadow,
but morning will break
on glorious battlements.

Hard the extremity of China,
of India and of Scotland,
bitter the loss of Spain,
where the great dead are;
hard the case of Italy,
of Germany and of France,
and the folly of England
that puts the poor to extremity.

Connolly is in Ireland
rising above agony,
Maclean in Scotland
a pillar on the heights;
Liebknecht in Germany
dead but undying,
and Lenin in Russia,
destination of great judgements.

*   *   *

I heard a cry in the mountains,
the liberty-shout of the people rising.

On the peaks around
were the living dead and their triumph
Toussaint, More, Lenin, Marx,
Liebknecht, Connolly, Maclean,
and many a proud spirit
extinguished in the extremity of Spain.

A thousand years was like a drift
of mist lost in the firmament.
The great Clio was ever rising,
a hundred thousand years paltry in her sight.
It was she who saw the Cuillin,
rising on the other side of anguish.

All proceeds from this publication go to Red Sunday School.

Red Sunday School is a space for children and young people to think for themselves, play with freedom, question the world around them, and change it. Organised by a group of communists, socialists and trade unionists on the principles of solidarity, the School provides tools and resources for the creative exploration of nature, culture and society from a radical perspective, and encourages active participation in the great struggles of our day: anti-racism, the climate crisis, feminism, and the revolutionary transformation of capitalism. Red Sunday School sets out to be an antidote to current mainstream education focused on producing workers ready to compete in the marketplace, regardless of the mental and physical costs to young people.

Red Sunday School meets on the last Sunday of the month in Kinning Park, Glasgow – where John Maclean used to teach. All children aged 0-12 are welcome!

www.tapsalteerie.co.uk

Tapsalteerie is an award-winning poetry publishing house based in rural Aberdeenshire. We produce an eclectic range of publications with a focus on new poets, translation, collaborations and innovative writing.